Cloud Computing and AWS Introduction

Docker | AWS Cloud Computing Platform | Serverless Computing | Virtualization | Virtual Machine | Hypervisor | IaaS | PaaS | SaaS | FaaS | DaaS | EC2 | IAM | S3 | AWS Security

SK Singh

AWS, Kafka, Hadoop, Unix, Oracle, Java Certified
Founder, Software, Cloud, Data Engineer

For my wife Daisy and children Pragya and Priti.

Preface

"Life is a journey, and the road we travel has twists and turns which sometimes lead us to unexpected places and unexpected people. But in turn, it always leads us to our destination." - Igwe Daniel Kelechi.

In Mar 2014, I got an email from a well-known publisher to write a book on AWS. I assume that the publisher might have found out from my LinkedIn profile that I was certified in AWS. I had my first AWS certification in Dec 2013. At that time, it was a little difficult to pass the AWS Solutions Architect certification exam as certification preparation-related resources and materials were not many. Unfortunately, I had to decline the request because of not getting my employer's consent.

Recently [2021], I was preparing a course on Udemy: "Introduction to Cloud Computing and AWS." When I published the videos, I realized that some add-on content was needed to complement the videos to understand better and retain the knowledge. Then, I decided to write some notes to help the students to learn more about the topics.

Then after a few weeks, writing supplementary notes for all the videos, it seemed to me that I had enough material to convert those notes into a book. So, I planned to write a book on the same topic, thinking it would be easy as I have good material.

I soon hit some challenges as I had little experience writing any book. However, any journey with friends and people who have already traveled the path makes it easy, even the more challenging terrain. This statement applied to me. Support from my friends and encouragement from my seniors made this process a little smoother, I guess.

Many of my close friends either helped directly by reviewing and providing feedback whenever I approached to seek their input and advice or indirectly helped, supported, and encouraged throughout the book's progress.

I would like to thank my close friends Adi Bhandaru (Cloud Migration, Global Program Delivery Portfolio Lead), Anjaiah Methuku, Anubhav Srivastava (Lead Engineer, AOL, Author of Java 9 regular expressions), Dmitry Doronin (Sr. Software Engineer, Dataminr), Kumar Rajesh (Director, Regulatory Services, ArisGlobal), Nick Sandru (DevOps Engineer, Apple), Nick Selya (JPMC), Roberto Dockery (VP, Morgan Stanley), Saurabh Banerjee (Director, Data Engineering, Publicis Sapient), Shailendra Dixit (Tech Manager), SooBok Shin (Software Engineer, Google), Sushim Dalbehera (Sr. Data Analytics Practitioner), Vishal Tandon (VP, JPMC) for their support, feedback, positive reinforcement, and encouragement.

I would also like to thank my two previous bosses Vinod Kumar (Executive Director, JPMC) and Jack Greene (Project Manager for a state government in the US Northeast), for their support and encouragement.

This acknowledgment will not be complete without thanking my close friends, Sharad Sharma (VP, JPMC), Ashok Pandey, and Dr. Vimal Mishra (Director, IERT Allahabad, India). They continuously provided their support, encouragement, and feedback from the very beginning in every step of publishing the book.

SK Singh
Dec 14th, 2021

Abstract

The word *cloud* in the term *cloud computing* is a metaphor for the Internet. Thus, cloud computing is essentially Internet-based computing. Internet-based computing is an extension of the classic client-server processing paradigm. As you can see, since cloud computing is Internet-based computing, cloud computing is more of a marketing term like JavaScript, which is not at all related to the Java programming language.

Though *cloud computing* (or Internet-based computing) extends the classic client-server-based computing model, there are distinct differences. And these differences make cloud computing stand out in its own unique way to become a new modern computing paradigm.

Let's discuss some unique differences. The classic client-server-based computing model is typically used in a LAN (Local Area Network) environment. Since the traditional client-server-based computing model's processing scope with respect to request/response is limited within LAN, cloud computing -- Internet-based computing (an extension of client-server computing) -- increases the scope of processing to make it global. It means cloud computing processes requests across the globe from anywhere, wherever the Internet is available. Another important distinct aspect of cloud computing (with respect to traditional client-server computing) is the availability of massive computing resources, which can be made available on-demand at any time from anywhere.

In Part I, we will understand cloud computing, its related terms, and many related foundational cloud computing concepts in more detail. We will also learn about advanced cloud computing concepts such as virtualization, serverless computing, and Docker. This part will help build a solid foundation on cloud computing, which is essential to learning any cloud computing platform such as AWS, Microsoft Azure, or Google Cloud platform.

In Part II, we will learn about Amazon Web Services. Amazon Web Services (AWS) started around 2005. From its cloud computing platform, AWS provides services such as infrastructure, platform, and software services to millions of customers worldwide. Organizations can build all sorts of applications on the AWS platform using its services. Also, to reduce the cost of their on-prem data center, they can use its infrastructure, storage, and other services to migrate their on-prem data center to the AWS cloud platform.

In Part II, First, we will learn about AWS Global Cloud Infrastructure, which is the backbone of AWS and responsible for delivering scalable cloud services securely and reliably, ensuring clients' data and assets are available, safe, and not compromised. In addition to AWS Global Cloud Infrastructure, we will also learn about EC2 (AWS service to launch virtual servers), IAM (AWS service to manage users), and S3 (AWS storage service). These are popular and sort of foundational services with respect to learning AWS as beginners. In the end, we will understand about AWS cloud computing platform, in which we will learn about many important AWS services at a high level, which can be helpful in AWS certification exams.

We will learn using examples, pictures (wherever possible), and hands-on where applicable. There is a reference of YouTube video(s) at the end of each chapter to help aid learning. These videos can be handy, particularly when doing hands-on learning.

Table of Contents

Take a chance! All life is a chance. The man who goes farthest is generally the one who is willing to do and dare. -- Dale Carnegie

Introduction

Learning any new engineering topic is fun yet challenging at times, particularly if it is less to do with extending the already known concepts. Understanding cloud computing and AWS, in my opinion, fits into this narrative.

Nonetheless, I hope you will find this book helpful in understanding cloud computing and AWS. In this book, we will learn almost all introductory foundational concepts related to cloud computing and AWS. Once we have got a solid foundation in cloud computing, then, in the second part, the book starts with what AWS is and goes into detail about many aspects of AWS with an introductory perspective.

The first part of the book is about the introduction to cloud computing and the second part is about the introduction to AWS. A brief summary of what is included in each chapter is as follows.

Chapter 1: What is Cloud Computing The book starts with what cloud computing is and many different cloud computing related terms. By the end of the first chapter, we should have gained a good conceptual understanding of cloud computing, cloud services, cloud computing platforms, and cloud service providers.

Chapter 2: Cloud Computing Platform Types The next chapter is about cloud computing platform types or cloud computing types. In this chapter, we will learn about the different main cloud computing platform types such as infrastructure-as-a-service, platform-as-a-service, and software-as-a-service.
Additionally, we will also get an overview of some modern cloud computing types, such as data-as-a-service (becoming a new paradigm to deliver data products), desktop-as-a-service, and function-as-a-service, which is getting popular nowadays in some business domains.

Chapter 3: Cloud Computing Deployment Models The following chapter is about different cloud computing deployment models. Cloud computing deployment models mainly deal with the management and accessibility of computing resources.
In this chapter, we will learn about each cloud computing deployment model such as public, private, hybrid, including community and multi-cloud. Finally, we will also understand multitenancy, which is a common term in cloud computing.

Chapter 4: Cloud Applications Deployment Models The next chapter is about deploying applications on the cloud computing platform. This chapter is helpful if you are involved in a cloud migration or modernization project.

Chapter 5: Cloud Computing Advantages The following chapter is about the advantages of cloud computing.

Chapter 6: Virtualization, Virtual Machine, and Hypervisor The next chapter is about virtualization, virtual machines, and hypervisors.

Chapter 7: Serverless Computing The following chapter is about serverless computing. We will get a good understanding of serverless computing, which is getting popular nowadays.

Learning serverless computing in cloud computing is essential nowadays with the inclusion of function-as-a-service components in most cloud-based modern architectures. In this chapter, we also learn about serverless stack, AWS serverless services, and other related serverless topics.

Chapter 8: Docker Introduction The next chapter is about Docker. This is a hands-on section. We will take a use case of running a web server using a docker container to understand Docker better. We will also learn many common docker commands from a DevOps perspective.
Once we have gained a solid understanding of cloud computing, then we start learning AWS.

Chapter 9: What is AWS? First, in this chapter, we will understand what AWS is and its overview. Then, we will understand how it compares with its competitors, the types of services it provides, why AWS is so popular.

Chapter 10: AWS Account Then the next chapter is about the AWS account. In this chapter, we will learn how to sign up for an AWS account, how to set up a budget alert, best practices for an AWS root account, how to secure AWS account using MFA, AWS free tier, AWS Billing & Cost Management Dashboard, and how to access AWS platform.

Chapter 11: AWS Cloud Infrastructure The following chapter is about AWS cloud infrastructure, which is the foundation of the AWS cloud platform with respect to its infrastructure. We will also learn about AWS Regions, and AWS Availability Zones, which are essentially AWS data centers related concepts.

Chapter 12: Elastic Compute Cloud (EC2) Introduction The next chapter is about EC2 (Elastic Compute Cloud), which is AWS IaaS type of service to launch virtual servers on AWS. First, we will learn what EC2 is. Next, we will learn how to launch an EC2 instance and set up a web server on EC2.

Chapter 13: Identity and Access Management (IAM) Introduction The following chapter is about IAM (Identity and Access Management). IAM is used to create and manage AWS users. In this chapter we will learn how to create an AWS user, attach an IAM policy, and generate keys, which is required to access AWS programmatically.

Chapter 14: Simple Storage Service (S3) Introduction The next chapter is about S3 (Simple Storage Service). It is a very popular AWS service. First, we will get an introduction to S3. Then, we will learn how to create a bucket on S3 and upload objects on S3.

Chapter 15: AWS Security and Compliance The following chapter is about an introduction to AWS security and compliance. This chapter will provide a high-level understanding of how AWS approaches the security and compliance of deployed applications.

Chapter 16: AWS Cloud Computing Platform This chapter provides an introduction to the AWS cloud computing platform covering many popular AWS services.

Chapter 17: Cost-Benefit Analysis The final chapter is about cost-benefit analysis of moving to a cloud platform. This chapter will also be helpful to synthesize your learning from previous chapters.

You will also find references to YouTube videos at the end of each chapter. These videos will further help in making learning easier.

This was the introduction and high-level summary of what is covered in each chapter. Let's start with the first chapter: what is cloud computing? Happy learning!

Part I: Cloud Computing

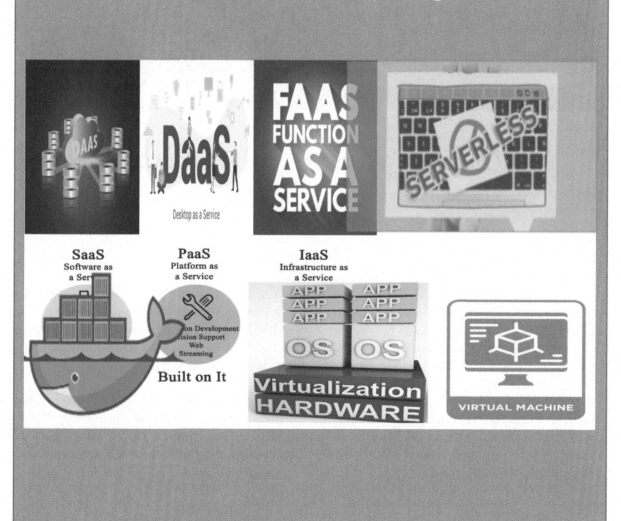

Chapter 1. What is Cloud Computing?

"Every kid coming out of Harvard, every kid coming out of school now thinks he can be the next Mark Zuckerberg, and with these new technologies like cloud computing, he actually has a shot." -- Marc Andreessen

AWS is a leading cloud provider -- according to the 2021 Gartner Magic Quadrant for Cloud Infrastructure & Platform Services -- with over a million customers of different types in around 200 countries. Moreover, AWS or any cloud provider's underpinning architecture is based on cloud computing. Therefore, the first and most important learning is a solid foundational and conceptual understanding of cloud computing as a cloud practitioner.

But before cloud computing, we will discuss some background, mainly traditional IT infrastructure, the reasoning, and motivation for the emergence of cloud computing. Then, we will start with what cloud computing is. In addition, in this chapter, we will also learn about many cloud computing related terms such as cloud computing platform, cloud service, and cloud computing platform provider.

Traditional IT infrastructure

Figure 1.1 Traditional IT

In the late 90s, with the dot com boom, we saw so many startups. Some of them have become big names now, such as Amazon Google. However, most of those startups have started from the so-called garage. First, they started with a few servers. Then, as their user base started increasing, they needed more machines to scale up their business.

Then, to handle the scalability issue, or in other words, to maintain system performance with the matching workload on the system, they moved their server infrastructure from garage to office, where they set up their servers in a so-called computer room or server room. That helped them overcome network bandwidth, power supply, and AC challenges when running the business with more servers.

When the user base increased further, they needed to scale further again. To manage the scalability, issue this time, they moved their servers or IT infrastructure to data centers. These data centers have more computing resources, power, air conditioning, security, and other related things that run 24x7 operations of 100s or 1000s servers.

Challenges with Data Center

Paying rent for hosting servers on data centers

Spacing is limited

Fixing, upgrading, or maintenance takes time

Need team to manage and monitor servers

What about if any natural disaster happens

Figure 1.2 challenges with data center

But still, there are challenges and issues with data centers, and what are those? And is there a better solution for this?

Let's talk about them. Depending on how much space you require for your servers, it costs a lot. And there are reasons for the cost as data centers provide 24 x 7 power supply, AC, maintenance, and security. So, it's obvious there will be a cost to all these services.

There is limited space – each data centers have some limited capacity. Even though data centers have a vast area, the space is limited. If you need to upgrade servers or do some maintenance, you will have to go to the data center (in many cases) to have the part replaced or do an upgrade, etc. You also need to manage and maintain servers 24x7. There is a single point of failure. What if any natural disaster happens?

So, the bigger general question is -- do we have a solution for all these challenges? Is there any other solution besides leveraging data centers for IT infrastructure? And the answer is: Cloud Computing. So, let's start with cloud computing.

What is Cloud Computing?

Before understanding the term **cloud computing**, it is important to know about the word "**cloud**" as this is an interesting word in this term. Interestingly, the word "**cloud**" in the term cloud computing is not related to the literal cloud-- at all. **Instead, the word "cloud" in cloud computing is a metaphor for the Internet.** Thus, cloud (as a metaphor for Internet) computing refers to Internet-based computing in which IT resources are delivered on-demand with pay-as-you-go pricing model.

Using cloud computing, organizations (cloud computing providers) offer services such as virtual machines (compute resource that uses software instead of a physical computer), virtual storage (storage pool formed by combining multiple network storage devices), and many other types of software applications (or services) over the Internet. So, for example, if you would like to set up a Linux virtual machine, and if you have an account with a cloud provider, you can launch it within a few minutes – just by using the web browser. And start using the Linux VM as you would use any regular physical Linux machine, for example, setting up a web server, database, or any other regular use of Linux machine you do.

In addition to virtual servers, cloud computing providers can also offer virtual storage. For example, if you need extra storage to store large collection of media files, you can use cloud computing provider's storage service to store them – very fast. You just need an account with the cloud provider and a web browser -- no need to shop around to buy the storage and waste additional time to set up the device, such as installing a driver before using the storage.
On the other hand, using cloud computing, cloud computing users such as organizations can develop and offer software applications (for example, Gmail, Office365, Facebook) or other related services.

In the above discussion, we learned about the term **cloud computing, cloud computing providers,** and **cloud computing users.**

Based on the above discussion, we can see that to launch a virtual machine or get virtual storage, we only need an account with the cloud provider and a web browser. In other words, cloud computing offerings (the common term is services) are provided over the Internet. Nonetheless, in general, there is nothing special about hardware. Cloud computing's underpinning hardware is the same type of physical server, storage, and network used in on-prem datacenters.

Figure 1.3 what is cloud computing

Then, the question comes how cloud computing differs from classic (non-cloud) computing. The main difference is that cloud computing uses cloud architecture. The cloud architecture enables technology components to combine to help build a cloud that can perform resource pooling through virtualization – running virtual machines as an abstraction layer

Figure 1.4 what is cloud computing

over a physical machine. In other words, cloud architecture helps organize and consolidate massive hardware such as computing resources, storage, and network -- to form resource pooling – and make it available over the Internet.

You may be thinking why there is so much talk about cloud computing. As you have noticed in the above discussion, cloud computing has many advantages (chapter 5 for details). One aspect of the advantages is, though organizations have been developing, delivering, and managing software for many decades, cloud computing has made this process of developing, delivering, and managing software to end users -- globally --much faster and relatively cheaper (cheaper may not always be true). The reason is that hardware infrastructure, software tools, and other whole hosts of things required for software development, testing, and deployment can be easily and quickly acquired and set up very fast. Additionally, it could be less expensive --- cloud providers nowadays offer various pricing models.

Though cloud computing has many advantages, it may not be appropriate for all use cases. Therefore, you will still need to do your homework if cloud computing is advantageous for your use case or organization.

Let's talk about a formal definition of cloud computing. According to Special Publication SP 800 – 145 [Sept 2011, Peter Mell (NIST), Tim Grance (NIST)] from The National Institute of Standards and Technology (NIST) of the United States.

Cloud computing is a model for enabling ubiquitous, convenient, on-demand network access to a shared pool of configurable computing resources (e.g., networks, servers, storage, applications, and services) that can be rapidly provisioned and released with minimal management effort or service provider interaction. This cloud model is composed of five essential characteristics, three service models, and four deployment models.

There are some keywords to notice in the NIST definition of cloud computing. These are: on-demand network access, shared pool of configurable computing resources, rapidly provisioned and released. On the other hand, in the traditional classic on-premises data center, the computing, storage, and network resources are bought, set up, and permanently configured by the customers in maximum capacity regardless of how much the actual need for help is. Depending on the business season, this resource allocation may be less. In that case, resources are wasted. However, there is also a possibility that the resources cannot meet demand. In that case, there is the chance of reducing service quality and the risk of losing customers because of quality concerns. There is no demand concept, sharing of the resource pool, and rapid on-demand provision in a classic on-premises data center. Another important point to keep in mind is that cloud computing is predicated upon the idea of purchasing "services" based on the needs of customers -- on-demand -- and stop, close the service, or terminate when you are done with the usage.

Cloud Computing Platform

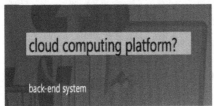

Figure 1.5 cloud computing platform

Now we know about the term cloud computing. There is another related term, cloud computing platform. The back-end system providing services is called a cloud computing platform.

Cloud Services (Web Services)

Another related term is cloud services -- also commonly called web services. Services provided by the cloud computing platform are called cloud services, for example, Gmail, Office365.

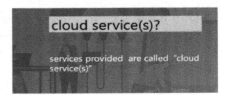

Figure 1.6 cloud services

Cloud Computing Platform Provider

Figure 1.7 cloud platform provider

We know the terms cloud computing, cloud computing platform, and cloud services (web services). Another related term to know is cloud computing platform provider. Cloud providers such as AWS, Google, Microsoft, IBM, Oracle, Salesforce, SAP, and others that provide cloud services from their cloud computing platform are called cloud computing platform providers (also commonly called cloud services providers or cloud providers). AWS, Google, Microsoft are the leading cloud computing platform providers.

As a side note, sometimes you will notice that the word "computing" may be missing in some casual or informal discussion of cloud computing. For example, you might hear cloud service(s) as opposed to cloud computing service(s), cloud provider(s) as opposed to cloud computing provider(s), or cloud platform(s) as opposed to cloud computing platform(s). But that doesn't change their semantics.

Software Quality Attributes

As a software professional, it is essential to have a good understanding of software quality attributes. Knowledge of software quality attributes becomes even more critical in a distributed computing environment such as cloud computing. The reasons are, there are so many variables: uneven load requests, the network could go down; there could be a bandwidth issue, latency issue; any cloud resource could go down. There are so many variables to consider, and these variables are often detrimental to the software's overall performance. If these variables are handled well, performance could go up, and the performance could go down if not noticed or not handled well.

What are Software Quality Attributes?

What are software quality attributes? Software quality attributes are features of the software by which we can measure its performance, for example, how reliable it is, how available it is, or how scalable it is. There are many quality attributes, but the main ones are usability, maintainability, modifiability, extensibility, portability, testability, flexibility, reusability, reliability, availability, and scalability. Depending on the kind of software and the service level agreements (SLA), some quality attributes are more important than others.

With respect to cloud computing, the important software quality attributes to consider are scalability, availability, and reliability. It's critical to understand them to handle performance-related issues in cloud computing. Therefore, we will discuss these -- scalability, availability, and reliability -- quality attributes.

Availability, Reliability

First, let's understand availability and reliability. Availability is a measure of the percentage of the time the system is in operable condition. On the other hand, reliability measures how long the system performs its intended function without breaking it down.

Say you have a machine that shuts down once in one hour, and it's down for 6 min before starting to become operable again. In that case, the machine availability is (60 - 6) / 60 = 90%; and it has the reliability of 1 hour because it can go down once within an hour. If the machine or software goes down but comes back immediately by rebooting or restarting itself, it can be considered highly available.

Just keep this in mind. A reliable system has high availability, but an available system may not be reliable.

Scalability

Scalability is the other important attribute in cloud computing. Scalability is a crucial quality attribute to pay attention to about software, particularly more in cloud computing, where request load is uneven much of the time.

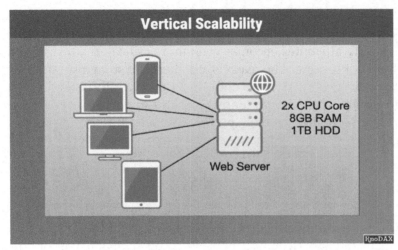

Having said this, what is scalability in software? Scalability in software refers to the quality attribute of the software that **measures the system's ability to perform as the load or the number of requests increases.** If the software performs without degradation of its performance as stated in its service level agreement, then it is considered scalable. On the other hand, if the system performance is impacted negatively, it is called

Figure 1.8 webserver machine handling requests

If we didn't manage scalability, the performance of the software would degrade if the load on the system increased. For example, suppose we deployed a simple e-commerce web application on a machine with 2x CPUs with 8 GB RAM. Say the application can handle 100 concurrent requests per second. Suppose due to some deal, the traffic on the system has increased. If we didn't manage the increase in the request, the application's performance would degrade – which means the system will start to behave poorly as it needs to process more than 100 concurrent requests per second. This could cause the CPU / RAM/ IO utilization to reach its maximum limit. As a result, the system would stop processing any further requests. This type of system can be called **non-scalable**.

The next obvious question is how to maintain the same performance or make the system scalable. For example, how to make the web application, in the example, scalable to process more than 100 concurrent requests per second without degradation in performance.

There are two approaches to managing software scalability: horizontal scalability and vertical scalability.

Vertical Scalability

To make a system vertical scalable, we replace the existing system with a higher configuration system or increase the existing system RAM, CPU, and HDD.

Let's understand vertical scalability with an example, as shown in the picture above. We have deployed a simple e-commerce web application on a machine with 2xCPUs with 8 GB RAM and a hard disk of 1 TB. The application can handle 100 concurrent requests per second.

Now suppose that the number of concurrent requests has increased during some time of the day on some special days. This is causing performance issues such as orders are not fulfilling, the customers are leaving the site and going to the competitor, or we are getting too many customers' support calls.

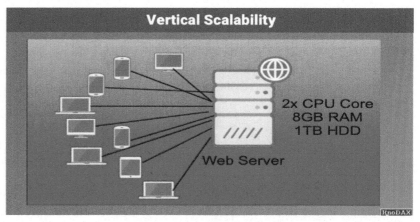

Figure 1.9 vertical scalable webserver machine

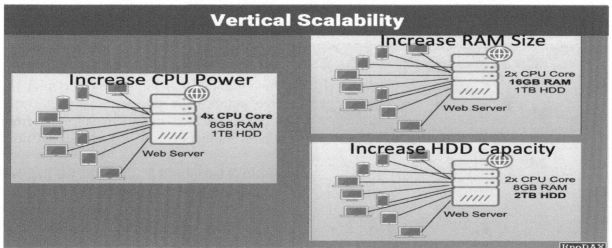

Figure 1.10 options to make a machine vertically scalable

To make the system horizontally scalable, we can increase RAM, increase the CPU clock speed, or increase HDD capacity depending on the performance analysis.

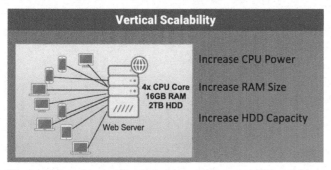

In summary, to make a system horizontally scalable, we increase the system's capacity on which the software is running. Or we can migrate the software to an entirely new machine that is more powerful in terms of CPU, RAM, or HDD – as you can notice in the picture, for example.

Figure 1.11 various options to make a machine vertically scalable

Making the system scalable by applying the vertical scalability technique was a typical pattern before the inclusion of stateless web services in modern software architecture.

Horizontal Scalability

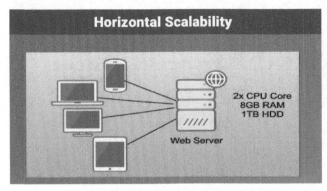

Figure 1.12 webserver handling requests

To manage the scalability of the software using the horizontal scalability, instead of increasing the system resources or migrating the software on a server, we distribute the requests on multiple servers to maintain the software performance. For example, in the use case which we are considering as an example, we have deployed a simple e-commerce web application on a machine with 2x CPUs with 8 GB RAM, and the application can handle 100 concurrent requests per second.

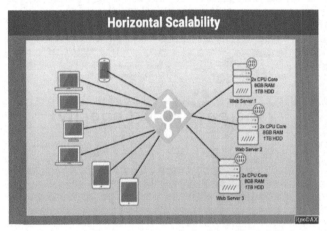

Figure 1.13 webserver setup for horizontally scalable

Say if the number of requests is increasing and we need to manage the scalability using the horizontal scalability, we can deploy the web application on, for example, three separate machines of the same type and front it with another device -- called load balancer.

The load balancer will distribute the requests -- depending on the type of load balancer -- on all the machines; thus, we can maintain the system performance when the load increases.

In other words, in a horizontally scalable solution, the software is deployed on multiple servers. And the request will be handled depending on the load of the servers and the type of load balancer. In other words, a single server will not be flooded with all the new requests as requests are distributed among the assigned servers by the load balancer, thus maintaining the system's expected performance.

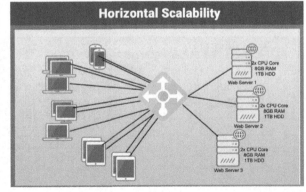

Figure 1.14 horizontally scalable webserver handling more requests

Summary

To summarize, the word cloud in cloud computing is used as a metaphor. Cloud computing refers to Internet-based computing. The back-end cloud computing system is called a cloud computing platform, and services provided by the cloud computing platform are called cloud services or web services. Providers such as AWS, Google, and Microsoft offering cloud services from their cloud computing platform are called cloud computing platform providers or cloud services providers.

References:

list of top cloud providers:
https://www.zdnet.com/article/the-top-cloud-providers-of-2021-aws-microsoft-azure-google-cloud-hybrid-saas/

Related YouTube Video
What is Cloud Computing: https://youtu.be/lr7oo_S_3jo

Chapter Review Questions

For the questions given below, please mark them if they are true or false.

1. The word "cloud" in cloud computing is used as a metaphor for "the Internet." True / False

2. The term "cloud computing" refers to Internet-based computing. True / False

3. Cloud computing is essentially about providing cloud services over the Internet. True / False

4. The cloud architecture enables cloud providers to organize and consolidate massive hardware, such as computing resources, storage, network, and software, to make it available over the Internet. True / False

5. AWS, Google, and Microsoft are also cloud providers because they provide public cloud services. True / False

6. The back-end system which is providing cloud services is called a "cloud computing platform." True / False

7. Availability and Reliability are the same concept just two different names. True/ False

8. An elastic system adds or removes resources based how it has been configured. True / False

Please select the correct answer from the given choices for the questions below.

9. What is cloud computing?

    a.   Cloud computing means providing virtual servers over the Internet.

b. Cloud computing means providing virtual storage over the Internet.

c. Cloud computing means providing software as a service over the Internet

d. All the above

10. Which of the following options is the feature of cloud computing?

a. Metered billing model

b. On-demand service

c. Scalability

d. All the above

11. Which of the following organizations is not a cloud service provider?

a. Google

b. Apple

c. Microsoft

d. Amazon

12. Which of the following statements is true?

a. Cloud computing and distributed computing are the same terms – two different names.

b. Cloud computing and distributed computing are not related concepts at all.

c. Cloud computing is conceptually distributed computing.

d. All distributed applications are based on cloud computing.

13. Which of the following statements is correct about cloud computing?

a. The word "cloud" in cloud computing is a metaphor.

b. Cloud computing providers provide services over the Internet.

c. Cloud computing abstracts out systems by pooling the shared resources.

d. All of the above

14. Which of the following statements is not correct?

a. Cloud computing can be a good choice for applications having highly scalable requirements.

b. Cloud computing can be a good choice for applications in need of reducing costs on their IT infrastructure.

c. Applications having strong low-latency, security, audit, and regulatory SLA can be the right fit for cloud computing.

d. Cloud computing can be a good choice for applications having high availability requirements.

15. Which of the following options about architecture is not related to cloud computing?

a. Micro-Services

b. Service-Oriented Architecture (SOA)

c. Monolith

d. None of them

16. Which of the following statements is true about cloud computing?

a. cloud computing provides virtual servers
b. cloud computing helps to get rid of on-prem data centers for computing needs
c. cloud computing helps cut costs on maintenance staff for 24x7 operations
d. all the above

17. Which of the following options is correct to make a system horizontally scalable?

a. Increase size of hard disk
b. Increase RAM size
c. Increase CPU clock speed
d. Add an additional server in the cluster

18. Which of the following options is correct to make a system vertically scalable?

a. Increase RAM size
b. Increase CPU clock speed
c. Increase size of disk
d. All of them

19. Which of the following options is the advantage of a flexible pricing model in cloud computing?

a. The flexible pricing model helps customer to get unlimited bandwidth.
b. The flexible pricing model enables customers to pay for what they use.
c. The flexible pricing model enables customers get storage free but will be changed for virtual servers.
d. The flexible pricing model enables customers to dynamically add resources when the resources are needed without any extra charge.

20. Which of the following statements is correct with respect to a use case of cloud computing?

a. A company has several hundreds of documents that need to be indexed in a few minutes.
b. A company needs a CRM solution as its customer base is increasing and it would like to provide the best customer service to its customers. However, it doesn't have time to build its home-grown solution for CRM as they don't have the resource and time for it.
c. A company engineering team needs servers to try out some POC type of work for 2-4 weeks. The servers are needed -- lay idle -- when POC is complete.
d. all of them

21. Which of the following statements is not correct?

a. Cloud computing can be a good choice for applications having highly scalable requirements.

b.   Cloud computing can be a good choice for applications in need of reducing costs on their IT infrastructure.

c.   Applications having strong low-latency, security, audit, and regulatory SLA can be the right fit for cloud computing.

d.   Cloud computing can be a good choice for applications having high availability requirements.

22. A startup company has developed a web application that is doing extremely well with local customers. Looking at the popularity of the software, the company is thinking of rollout this application worldwide. The company engineering president is thinking to deploy this application on a cloud computing platform. Which of the following attributes of cloud computing is helpful to decide if cloud computing is the right choice for deploying the application on the cloud platform?

   a. Availability
   b. Scalability
   c. Flexible pricing such as pay-as-you-go or metered pricing model
   d. All the above

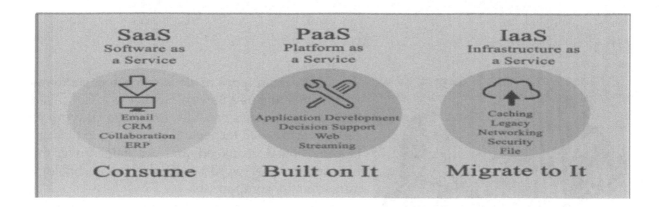

Chapter 2. Cloud Computing Platform Types

"The interesting thing about cloud computing is that we've redefined cloud computing to include everything that we already do. I can't think of anything that isn't cloud computing with all of these announcements." -- Lary Ellison, chairman of Oracle Corporation and chief technology officer

As we learned in the previous chapter, a **cloud computing platform** is a back-end system that provides services over the Internet. The question is what kind of services the platform provides. For example, does the cloud computing platform provide Gmail, Office 365? Does it provide virtual servers, virtual storage? Or, does the cloud computing platform offer database services over the internet? Depending on the cloud computing platform's kind of service, it has been categorized into a type. This categorization is called **cloud computing platform types** or **cloud computing types**.

Continuing further on our discussion about cloud computing platforms: **cloud computing platform,** the back-end system providing services, is a general term. To be more specific, there are three main types of **cloud computing platforms: Infrastructure-as-a-Service (IaaS), Platform-as-a-Service (PaaS),** and **Software-as-a-Service (SaaS).**

In addition to these main ones, other modern cloud computing platform types have emerged recently, such as **Data-as-a-Service (DaaS), Desktop-as-a-Service,** and **Function-as-a-Service (FaaS).** These modern cloud computing platform types, which provide more fine-grained kinds of services, are getting popular very fast. In this chapter, we will learn about different cloud computing platform types (cloud computing types).

Infrastructure-as-a-Service (IaaS)

What is IaaS?

Figure 2.1 cloud computing pyramid diagram

One of the main types of **cloud computing platforms** is **Infrastructure-as-a-Service**, which is also called **IaaS**, in short. IaaS provides foundational types of services also called **technology infrastructure** that can be provisioned, managed, and maintained over the Internet. In other words, IaaS provides technology infrastructure components.

For example, IaaS offers virtual servers, virtual storage, and virtual network as a service. As you can notice in the given picture, in the cloud computing pyramid diagram, IaaS is at the foundation. What it means is that IaaS acts as the foundation for the cloud computing platform.

Let's understand virtual servers in IaaS with a use case. Suppose we need three Linux machines to work on some proof-of-concept (POC) type of work, for example, to build your home-grown load balancer. And we know that once our POC is complete, we will not need those machines further, and we are students with a tight budget. In this situation, IaaS is one of the best options. We could use the IaaS offering from a cloud provider to launch virtual servers and work on our POC. Once the POC is complete, we can terminate the servers and not be charged by the providers anymore.

Figure 2.2 infrastructure-as-a-service

Like virtual servers, we can also utilize the virtual storage feature of IaaS in situations where, for example, it would be a cheaper or more viable option to use virtual storage than buying physical storage. Let's try to understand it with a use case. Suppose we need temporary storage of around 5TB to store some media files for about a month to share with our friends, and we don't want to use the other video hosting services because of our own decisions. In this situation, as you can realize, utilizing virtual storage from cloud providers would be a better feasible choice than buying physical storage. Once we decide that we don't need storage anymore, we can delete the media files, and the provider will not charge us.

IaaS Advantages

We got an understanding about what IaaS is. Let's try to understand IaaS fruitfulness. One of the advantages of the IaaS type of **cloud computing platform** is that it could eliminate an on-premises data center's buying, setup, and maintenance expense. It's an obvious advantage. When using IaaS -- to procure servers, storage, and network – depending on how much infrastructure you procure, you would be able to cut down huge on your on-premises data-center expenses.

Figure 2.3 IaaS advantages

Since IaaS helps reduce data-center expenses significantly, IaaS could be an excellent choice for smaller companies and startups that don't have the resources or time to set up their technology infrastructure. Not only does IaaS help reduce the setup cost of technology infrastructure, but IaaS also takes away the operational expense and the burden of day-to-day managing of computing infrastructure. For example, you can outsource day-to-day tasks such as taking backup, applying patches, ensuring that the system is secured (not a security risk) to the IaaS provider.

IaaS Examples

As we discussed that IaaS provides technology infrastructure components. Some concrete examples of IaaS are AWS EC2 (Elastic Compute Cloud) for virtual servers, AWS EBS (Elastic Block Store) for virtual storage, and AWS Internet gateway for the virtual network.

Figure 2.4 IaaS examples

For virtual servers, the AWS EC2 service is an example of an IaaS type of service. In other words, using the EC2 service, you can launch (AWS term of running virtual servers) Linux, Windows, or Mac virtual servers on AWS. For virtual storage, AWS EBS is an excellent example of an IaaS virtual storage service. EBS is an IaaS type of service as the service provides storage as a service.

We looked up virtual servers, virtual storage examples. With regards to the virtual network, AWS Internet gateway is an excellent example of a virtual network. AWS Internet gateway manages Internet access for the servers launched on AWS.

Other cloud providers also have IaaS types of services. However, since this book is more focused on AWS, you will find examples of AWS services instead of examples of services from the other cloud providers. To summarize, **IaaS** cloud computing type deals with technology infrastructure such as virtual servers, virtual storage, and virtual networks.

Platform-as-a-Service (PaaS)

What is PaaS?

Figure 2.5 cloud computing pyramid diagram

Platform-as-a-Service (PaaS) is another primary type of **cloud computing platform** or **cloud computing type**. **PaaS** provides platform technology infrastructure-related services, for example, databases, web servers, messaging, to build, test, and deploy software. In other words, **PaaS** offers complete development and deployment environment in the cloud.

To understand how **PaaS** relates to **IaaS**, let's visit the **cloud computing** pyramid diagram as you can notice that PaaS is above IaaS. What it means is that PaaS can utilize IaaS for its infrastructure-related needs. In other words, PaaS can fulfill its virtual servers, storage, and network-related needs from IaaS.

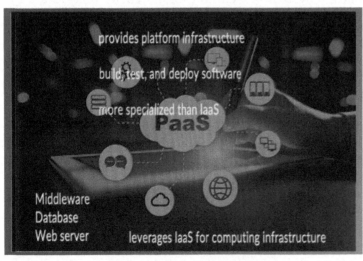

Figure 2.6 platform-as-a-service

Now we got the understanding that PaaS offers development and deployment-related services on the cloud. Let's try to understand PaaS with a use case example. Suppose you are VP engineering of a startup with a global team, and even for the local team members, you would like to have the flexibility of remote work. You have heard that platform-as-a-service is a cloud computing type where you can get complete development and deployment environment. So, the question is, what those tools, services, or platforms are that you could consider procuring for your team's software development needs using PaaS.

Depending on your needs, in PaaS computing type, you can find almost anything you require to set up a classic application software development environment. For example, PaaS can offer you IDE (Integrated Development Environment), source code management tools, and build tools. Moreover, in PaaS, you can also get databases, integration tools, web servers, ETL (Extract-

Transform-Load) tools, analytic tools, and many more on the cloud platform like AWS. To summarize, PaaS can help you get complete development and deployment-related services on the cloud.

PaaS Examples

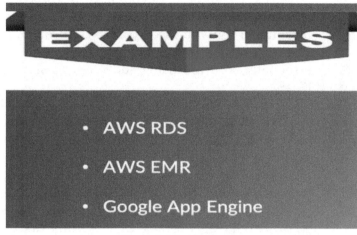

AWS has many PaaS services, such as AWS RDS (Relational Database Service), EMR (Elastic Map Reduce), to name a few. Google App Engine is also an excellent example of PaaS.

Let's discuss further PaaS examples, mainly what we can get on AWS. For IDE, AWS has Cloud9, a cloud-based integrated development environment that lets you write, run, and debug your code with just a browser. For the source code management system, you can use AWS CodeCommit, which is a secure, highly scalable, managed

Figure 2.7 PaaS examples

service that hosts private Git repositories. To build a data pipeline and schedule ETL jobs, you can use AWS Glue. Finally, to develop and manage your applications' Docker images, you can use AWS ECS.

There are many services on AWS that qualify for PaaS. The above ones are just examples to give you an overall understanding of PaaS.

To revise, PaaS provides complete development and deployment-related tools and services in the cloud. Moreover, these services can be accessed anytime on-demand from anywhere over the Internet. Thus, it eliminates in-house buying and setup of databases, web servers, development, and deployment-related tools and services.

Software-as-a-Service (SaaS)

What is SaaS?

Figure 2.8 what is SaaS

Have you used Gmail? Did you happen to watch movies on Netflix? Do you have a Facebook account? Does your workplace use Zoom for meetings? Have you used Microsoft Office 365? If your answer is "Yes" to any of these questions, essentially, you are using software-as-a-service (SaaS).

As IaaS and PaaS, SaaS is another main cloud computing platform or cloud computing type. If IaaS is about infrastructure, PaaS is about the platform – then SaaS is about software. In SaaS, essentially, software solutions are delivered as a service over the Internet. Therefore, SaaS software is mostly executed directly within a web browser. This feature of SaaS eliminates the need to install or download software to execute it.

For example, Gmail, Netflix, Facebook, Zoom, Microsoft Office 365 are some common examples of SaaS. There are countless examples of SaaS, but I'll limit it to a few to keep it simple. To illustrate further, to use Gmail, you don't need to install Gmail on your local computer. You just open a web browser, type the Gmail web URL in the address bar, and start using Gmail. On the same token, to watch a movie on Netflix, since Netflix is a SaaS solution or SaaS software, you don't need to install Netflix software on your local computer. Just open a web browser, type the Netflix web URL in the address bar, and you're ready to start watching movies on Netflix. As you can notice with these illustrations, that in SaaS, you don't need to install or download software to execute it.

SaaS is a very well-known type of cloud computing platform. The reason is SaaS is very visible to the common public usage wise. For example, as we know SaaS software such as Facebook, Netflix, Zoom, Microsoft Office 365 are very popular and have a global reach to millions of users. Additionally, with cloud computing, building SaaS applications have become relatively much faster, which further helps increase its popularity in the developer community.

Comparing SaaS with other main cloud computing types, if you look at the cloud computing pyramid diagram, SaaS is at the top. It means that if you are building SaaS solutions, you can use PaaS for platform-related needs and IaaS for infrastructure-related needs.

With respect to cost, SaaS software is typically licensed on a subscription basis. SaaS providers manage all the aspects of software, such as delivery and management, ensuring that service level agreement (SLA) is maintained. Thus, the software is available whenever or wherever the customer needs it, and it performs as per the service level agreement.

SaaS Advantages

In SaaS, we do not need to install any special software. SaaS software can be up and running quickly and can scale as needed. There is a substantial cost benefits for smaller or startup organizations in using SaaS.

Figure 2.9 SaaS advantages

Since SaaS is delivered over the Internet, we don't need to deploy or install any software on your local computer -- we can start using SaaS software as soon as we establish the connection using a web URL. In other words, it can be quickly up and running.

Furthermore, SaaS software can be easily scaled as needed. What it means, we wouldn't notice any performance degradation if traffic or the number of users increases.

In the late 90s, before cloud computing dominance, buying, and setting up enterprise software such as ERP, CRM, HR was very expensive. However, SaaS has made a significant difference in pricing, particularly for smaller or startup organizations, which could not afford to buy and set up expensive software such as ERP, CRM, HR, and many. In other words, the subscription-based pricing model of SaaS has made it much easier for smaller or startup organizations to use or subscribe to costly SaaS software to help grow their business.

If we were studying cloud computing in early 2000, then this chapter would have been completed by now. Because, for practical purposes, around that time, the cloud computing paradigm started, and IaaS, PaaS, SaaS are the only ones we needed to learn as far as cloud computing types are concerned.

Nonetheless, last 20 years, there have been lots of excellent engineering work have been done in the cloud computing field. As a result, cloud computing and its related cousins, such as web services and micro-services, are reaching maturity. Moreover, recently with technological advances and modernization, many new modern cloud computing types have emerged and joined the mainstream technology, for example, **Data-as-a-Service (DaaS), Desktop-as-a-Service (DaaS), Function-as-a-Service (FaaS)**. Additionally, many others have emerged as well, for instance, **Content-as-a-Service, Mobile-backend-as-a-Service, Network-as-a-Service, Security-as-a-Service**. However, these new types of services are out of the scope of this book. In the rest of this chapter, I'll touch upon **Data-as-a-Service, Desktop-as-a-Service, and Function-as-a-Service**, which we may come across working as professional engineers.

Data-as-a-Service (DaaS)

What is Data-as-a-Service (DaaS)?

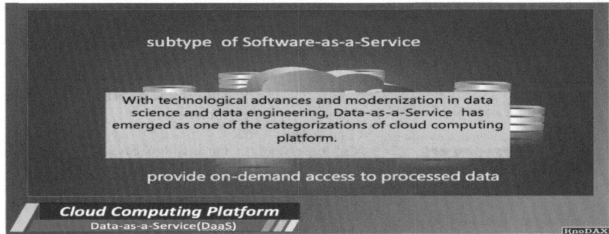

Figure 2.10 what is data-as-a-service

Software engineering is advancing very fast -- either to solve complex business and engineering problems or re-engineer already developed solutions. In other words, software engineers are continuously making and delivering better solutions for all stockholders.

Recently with modernization in data engineering, analytics, and web services, Data-as-a-Service, also called DaaS, has emerged as one of the categorizations of cloud computing platforms. Data-as-a-Service (DaaS) is a subtype of Software-as-a-Service. Essentially, DaaS is about offering on-demand access to processed data or data products.

Data-as-a-Service (DaaS) Advantages

Figure 2.11 DaaS advantages

Regarding data-as-a-service advantages, DaaS offers on-demand accessibility to processed data or data products from anywhere, along with cost-effectiveness and improved data quality.

One of the main advantages of data-as-a-service is that data products can be accessed on-demand from anywhere, which is a huge advantage. For example, in DaaS, users can pull or retrieve analytic reports related to all kinds of data anytime from anywhere, just by using a web browser. As we know in classic ETL shops, to get reports, users would have to wait for a successful run of ETL jobs at a pre-defined time, which is usually early morning or late night. However, in the case of DaaS, users can their reports on-demand from anywhere – essentially no long wait.

It also adds cost-effectiveness. With automated ETL jobs, once we have developed data pipelines and automated the process of data ingestion, data transformation, and data publishing with a web service endpoint, we save huge on your data products as these are the primarily repeatable type of work.

DaaS improves data quality as well as we can add test cases in the data pipelines to make sure that data products are producing the correct result.
To revise, data-as-a-service (DaaS) enables on-demand access to data products, improves data quality, and efficiency in cost and time to process data.

Desktop-as-a-Service (DaaS)

What is Desktop-as-a-Service (DaaS)?

If you have ever connected to your workplace system remotely using Citrix, you have already used desktop-as-a-service (DaaS). It is a subtype of software-as-a-service. Essentially, DaaS delivers virtual applications and desktop services over the Internet.

Figure 2.12 what is desktop-as-a-service

Using the desktop-as-a-service cloud computing type, we can use a remote desktop service to access desktop machines remotely.

The way desktop-as-a-service works is that DaaS providers host the backend virtual desktop infrastructure (VDI) and stream virtual desktops to nd is multi-tenant in nature like any other SaaS software. With regards to DaaS examples, the Citrix server is an excellent example of a desktop-as-a-service. You can use this service like any other cloud service via a web browser.

Desktop-as-a-Service (DaaS) Advantages

Figure 2.13 desktop-as-a-service advantages

Desktop-as-a-Service (DaaS) makes monitoring, auditing, securing, and managing desktop infrastructure easier and efficient, because of the centralization. In DaaS, clients don't need to install any software to use their desktops, as they can connect to their desktops just using a web browser.

Desktop-as-a-Service (DaaS) Examples

If your workplace uses desktop-as-a-service, you can connect to your workplace desktop remotely using a browser or some client. For example, you can use Citrix client to get full Windows-based virtual desktops. In this use case, essentially, you are leveraging desktop as a service.

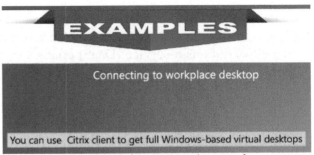

Figure 2,14 desktop-as-a-service examples

To summarize, desktop-as-a-service essentially delivers virtual applications and desktop services over the Internet, making monitoring, auditing, securing, and managing desktop infrastructure more manageable and efficient.

Figure 2.15 desktop-as-a-service summary

Function-as-a-Service (FaaS)

What is FaaS?

Function-as-a-Service (FaaS), synonymous with serverless computing, is another type of modern cloud computing platform or cloud computing type.

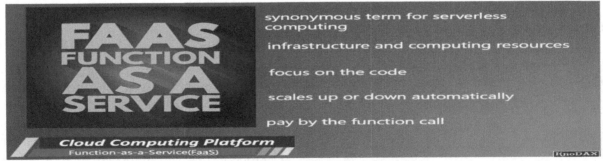

Figure 2.16 what is FaaS

So what does FaaS do? Essentially, in FaaS, users only need to focus on the code (write a Java class, for example) – not on the infrastructure (no need to set up JVM, for example). Users deploy the code having a function (Java class, for example), and the FaaS provider executes the code. The runtime environment is not only provided by the providers but managed as well.

FaaS Advantages

Figure 2.17 FaaS advantages

FaaS providers provide infrastructure and computing resources to functions without users setting up the infrastructure and computing resources to execute the process. Additionally, the execution environment scales up or down automatically. Because of the automatic theoretical unlimited scalability feature of FaaS, it is an excellent solution choice for method or function calls, which have a dynamic workload that fluctuates a lot. Moreover, one distinct advantage of FaaS is that we only pay for the computing resources used by function calls – essentially a pay-as-you-go-pricing model.

One of the main drawbacks of function-as-a-service is the execution time. Since process needs to have resource provisioned each time they run, there is a possibility of some performance lag.

FaaS Examples

One of the examples of function-as-service is AWS Lambda. For example, say we have an image processing function for generating thumbnail images. We can write the process in the language

Figure 2.18 FaaS examples

choices, such as Java, Python, and other supported languages by the cloud provider, and let AWS Lambda execute the function. In this use case, we only need to write a function for image processing and configure the computing resource requirement on AWS Lambda. Then, AWS Lambda will take care of the allocation of computing resources and run the image processing function.

Related YouTube Videos

Cloud Computing Types: https://youtu.be/DMePTTvmsZ0
Infrastructure-as-a-Service (IaaS) : https://youtu.be/UXGNafGjBQQ
Platform-as-a-Service (PaaS): https://youtu.be/mszigptiVQI
Software-as-a-Service(SaaS): https://youtu.be/yL5AhrTO6Is
Desktop-as-a-Service: https://youtu.be/MUqHwm5PRoc
Data-as-a-Service: https://youtu.be/32YvzBQYP9g
Function-as-a-Service (FaaS): https://youtu.be/Qs5EmkB5s_I

Chapter Review Questions

For the questions given below, please mark them if they are true or false.

1. SaaS software is mostly executed directly within a web browser. True / False
2. Function-as-a-Service (FaaS) is not a good solution choice for method or function calls, which have a dynamic workload that fluctuates a lot. True / False

Please select the correct answer from the given choices for the questions given below.

3. Which of the following types of cloud service does IaaS offer?

      a. Virtual Server
      b. Virtual Storage
      c. Virtual Network
      d. All of them

4. In Infrastructure-as-a-Service type of delivery model, which of the following resources is generally provided by cloud providers?

      a. Software Applications
      b. Virtual Network
      c. Virtual servers
      d. Middleware

5. In cloud computing, which of the following layers is used to provide software-as-a-service?

      a. application layer
      b. infrastructure layer
      c. data layer
      d. none of them

6. Which of the following providers is of software-as-a-service cloud computing type?

      a. data service provider
      b. application service provider
      c. internet service provider
      d. infrastructure service provider

7. A start-up software organization would like to test and deploy its software solutions on the cloud platform in order to save cost in avoid buying and maintaining expensive servers. The company is looking for a cloud provider which offers virtual servers provisioning and on-demand storage services. Which of the following cloud computing delivery models is the start-up company looking for?

      a. Software-as-a-Service
      b. Platform-as-a-Service
      c. Application-as-a-Service
      d. Infrastructure-as-a-Service

8. In which of the following distribution models, a software application is hosted on the cloud, and users can access the software using the Internet?

a. Software-as-a-Service
b. Platform-as-a-Service
c. Infrastructure-as-a-Service
d. all of them

9. Which of the following options is used to access Software-as-a-Service (SaaS) type of applications?

a. Web Browser
b. client software needs to be installed to access SaaS applications
c. command line
d. none of them

10. A cloud provider provides software tools and platforms to develop applications that can be run from the customer's environment. Which of the following cloud computing delivery models is used by the cloud provider?

a. Software-as-a-Service
b. Platform-as-a-Service
c. Infrastructure-as-a-Service
d. Desktop-as-a-Service

11. A web-based email application running in a cloud environment is an example of what type of cloud computing?

a. Software-as-a-Service
b. Platform-as-a-Service
c. Infrastructure-as-a-Service
d. all of them

12. Which of the following statements is correct with respect to a use case of cloud computing?

a. A company has several hundreds of documents that need to be indexed in a few minutes.
b. A company needs a CRM solution as its customer base is increasing and it would like to provide the best customer service to its customers. However, it doesn't have time to build its home-grown solution for CRM as they don't have the resource and time for it.
c. A company engineering team needs servers to try out some POC type of work for 2-4 weeks. The servers are needed -- lay idle -- when POC is complete.
d. all of them

13. Which of the following statements is true about an application service provider?

a. An application service provider uses the software-as-a-service delivery model to provide software as a service over the Internet.
b. The provider essentially provides virtual servers over the Internet
c. The provider provides platform-as-a-service.

d. all of them

14. You are a cloud engineer in a start-up organization. You have asked to provide access to virtual machines in a cloud environment. Which of the following cloud computing delivery models would you leverage?

    a. Platform-as-a-Service
    b. Infrastructure-as-a-Service
    c. Function-as-a-Service
    d. Software-as-a-Service

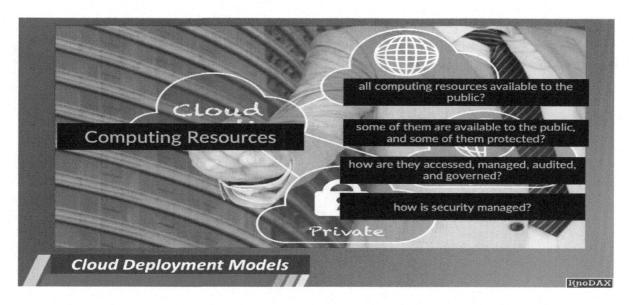

Chapter 3. Cloud Computing Deployment Models

"I don't need a hard disk in my computer if I can get to the server faster... carrying around these non-connected computers is byzantine by comparison." -- Steve Jobs, Late Chairman – Apple

When we talk about cloud computing, it's critical to understand computing resources in terms of their accessibility, management, audit, governance, and security. Understanding computing resources in terms of these aspects of cloud computing comes under the term cloud computing deployment model or cloud deployment model.

It's essential to understand about cloud computing deployment model because, as a solution architect, understanding this concept would help you choose appropriate architectural options regarding how to deploy your applications on the cloud. In this chapter, first, we will get a conceptual understanding of the cloud computing deployment model. Then we will learn about different cloud deployment models: public, private, hybrid, and community. Additionally, we will also understand multi-cloud, and multitenancy -- both are crucial terms of cloud computing.

What is Cloud Computing Deployment Model?

The cloud deployment model describes how a cloud computing platform is implemented, hosted and who has access to it. For instance, what is the accessibility of computing resources? Are all computing resources available to the public? Or not all -- only some of them are available to the public, and some computing resources are protected. How are computing resources accessed, managed, audited, or governed? How is the security of computing resources managed? Understanding computing resources in terms of these aspects of cloud computing comes under the term cloud computing deployment model (or cloud deployment model).

There are four types of cloud deployment models: public cloud, private cloud, hybrid cloud, and community cloud.

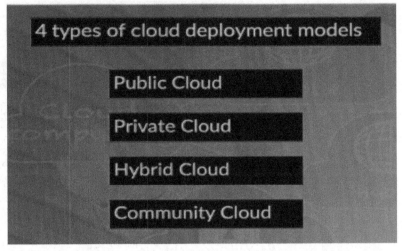

Figure 3.1 cloud deployment model types

Public Cloud

What is Public Cloud?

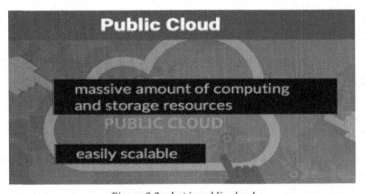

Figure 3.2 what is public cloud

A public cloud deployment model (or public cloud) provides on-demand availability of all kinds (for example, IaaS, PaaS, SaaS) of cloud services from across the world.

A public cloud, in general, has a massive amount of -- computing resources and storage -- easily available and is easily scalable.

A public cloud has easy accessibility compared to any other type of cloud. This is because public clouds, by nature of the **public,** are generally available to everyone. So, for example, if you would like to launch a virtual server on AWS (a public cloud provider), you just need to have an account with AWS, and you can easily and quickly launch a virtual server on AWS. Similarly, you can quickly get storage on a public cloud such as AWS.

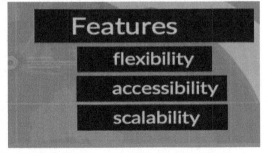

Figure 3.3 public cloud features

The main point to understand as it relates to accessibility is that getting cloud services from public cloud providers is relatively much more straightforward than getting cloud services in any other type of cloud deployment model (private, hybrid). The reason is that accessibility limits or permission issues are much lenient in the public cloud than in any other cloud deployment model.

Cloud Computing and AWS Introduction

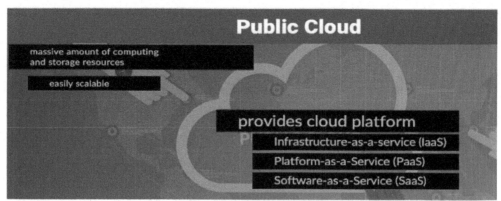

Figure 3.4 public cloud features

Public cloud providers generally provide cloud platforms for all main cloud computing types: Infrastructure-as-a-Service (IaaS), Platform-as-a-Service (PaaS), Software-as-a-Service (SaaS). For example, they provide infrastructure-as-a-service (IaaS), which means you can launch virtual servers on the cloud, such as Linux virtual servers, Windows virtual servers, or even macOS type of virtual servers on AWS. Furthermore, they provide platform-as-a-service (PaaS), which means, for example, you can get development and deployment software and tools on the cloud. Also, they provide software-as-a-service (SaaS), which means you can get application software solutions delivered over the Internet.

A **public** cloud is a recommended choice for developing cloud-based applications for globally distributed teams -- because the public cloud helps in team collaboration in terms of cloud resources. Moreover, once the application development is complete, if you would like to move the final application to a more secure private cloud, you can do that easily. Examples of public cloud providers are AWS, Google, Microsoft, IBM, Oracle, Salesforce, SAP, AWS, Google, Microsoft are the leading cloud providers.

Pros & Cons

Figure 3.5 public cloud pros & cons

A **public** cloud provides most of the advantages of cloud computing, such as the pay-as-you-go pricing model and on-demand availability of all kinds of cloud services from across the world.

The one main drawback of a public cloud is that the cloud provider owns the computing resources. And in that sense, there is a single point of failure if something goes wrong at the provider's end, for example, if the provider goes out of business.

Private Cloud

What is Private Cloud?

Figure 3.6 what is private cloud

It is like a **public** cloud, but a **private** cloud is most restrictive. A private cloud is sometimes also called an on-premises cloud solution if the cloud resources are within the organization's data center.

With respect to how a private cloud is like a public cloud, in a private cloud you can get all the public cloud features, such as on-demand availability of all kinds of cloud services from across the world. Additionally, like a public cloud, a private cloud also has massive computing resources and storage available, making it easily scalable -- but relatively lesser compared with a public cloud.

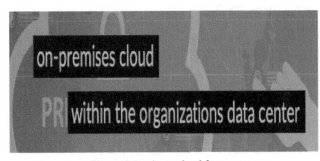

Figure 3.7 private cloud features

As we discussed, though private cloud is like public cloud, a private cloud is most restrictive and has tighter controls -- typically protected by firewalls. Because of stricter control and firewall protection, usually, a single organization utilizes a private cloud. Organizations with solid security and regulatory requirements such as banks, and healthcare providers prefer private cloud – particularly total on-premises cloud solutions.

There is an emerging trend of using colocation providers, in which the private cloud of an organization is set up inside a third-party datacenter. Thus, the organization, instead of having its own on-premises data center, is outsourcing to the third-party data center.

Pros & Cons

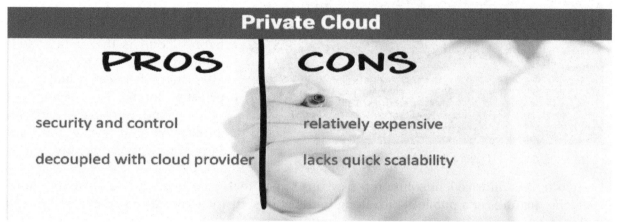

Figure 3.8 private cloud pros & cons

Security and control are the main advantages of a **private** cloud. For example, since a private cloud is behind a firewall, the private cloud makes it easier to restrict access to valuable assets.

With respect to the control advantage of private cloud, since an outside public cloud provider does not control a private cloud, there is no risk or a single point of failure if something goes wrong with the public cloud provider. This is a real plus, as in a private cloud, essentially, there is no dependency on public cloud providers -- the private cloud controls all computing resources. Another point about the controlling advantage of a private cloud is, a private cloud is recommended if regulatory needs are critical to controlling the environment.

Regarding its disadvantages, one of the disadvantages of the private cloud is cost. The company that owns a private cloud needs to bear the cost of the IT infrastructure of data centers and software. This cost factor makes private clouds less attractive compared to the public cloud. Another disadvantage is that increasing scalability in the private cloud is not as quick as in the public cloud because, in the private cloud, resources are in a limited capacity.

Hybrid Cloud

What is Hybrid Cloud?

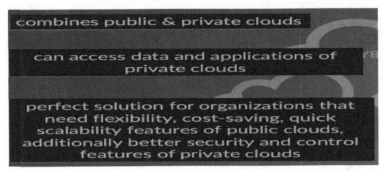

Figure 3.9 what is hybrid cloud

In simple words, it combines both public and private clouds. The main point to keep in mind about a hybrid cloud is that it is a cloud solution that allows seamless interaction between public and private clouds. For example, a public cloud can access data and applications of a private cloud, and the converse is also possible.

Therefore, it is an excellent solution for organizations that need flexibility, cost-saving, quick scalability features of a public cloud, along with better security and control features of a private cloud.

Types of Hybrid Clouds

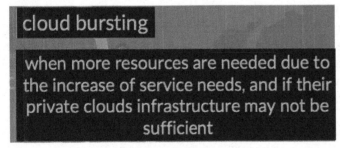

Figure 3.10 types of hybrid clouds

There are two types of hybrid clouds: **cloud bursting hybrid cloud** and the other one is **classic hybrid cloud**. In the bursting cloud type of hybrid cloud, organizations use private clouds to securely store their data and proprietary applications. However, when more resources are needed due to the increase of service needs, and if their private clouds infrastructure may not be sufficient, they look for public clouds and tap into public clouds resources to fulfill their increased service demands.

In a classic hybrid cloud, organizations store their data and proprietary applications on the private clouds. However, they outsource their non-critical applications to public clouds -- such as Microsoft office 365, or CRM solutions such as Salesforce. Also in a hybrid cloud, organizations can leverage multi-cloud architecture where organizations can use different cloud providers for their various cloud services' needs.

Pros & Cons

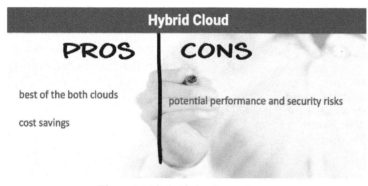

Figure 3.11 hybrid cloud pros & cons

A **hybrid cloud**'s main advantage is that we can leverage the best features of both types of clouds. For example, organizations can use private clouds to tightly secure and regulate their data. Furthermore, they can securely move them to public clouds such as AWS, for example, to leverage their analytical, machine learning services to build actionable insight solutions with cost and time efficiency.

Additionally, a hybrid cloud saves overall IT infrastructure cost because a public cloud can be used when scalability is needed. In addition to cost savings, many services are readily available on public cloud providers, which can be leveraged instead of developing your in-house solutions, for example, analytical services.

With regards to cons, since there is integration involved between private and public clouds. This integration can cause potential performance issues because of -- network latency and security risks -- as data are shared between public and private clouds.

Community Cloud

What is Community Cloud?

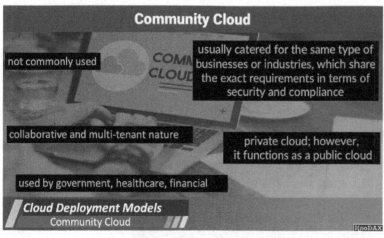

Figure 3.12 what is community cloud

Essentially, a **community cloud** is a private cloud, however, it functions as a public cloud. Community clouds are collaborative and multi-tenant in nature and usually catered for the same type of businesses or industries, which share the exact requirements in terms of security and compliance.

Though community clouds are not commonly used, they are typically used by government, healthcare, financial and other types of organizations.

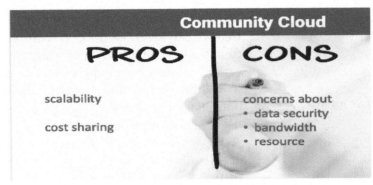

Community cloud's advantages are scalability are cost. They are more scalable compared to private clouds. Also, costs could be shared among the organizations using the community clouds.

Figure 3.13 community cloud pros & cons

Besides advantages, community clouds have some significant drawbacks because of sharing nature of this type of cloud. These are concerns about data security, bandwidth, and resource usage utilizations and prioritizations.

Multi-Cloud

In some cases, just one private, public, or hybrid doesn't fulfill all the cloud computing needs of organizations, and they resort to a multi-cloud model. The multi-cloud model involves private clouds and many public clouds. Though there are multi-clouds, all the clouds can be accessed from a single network.

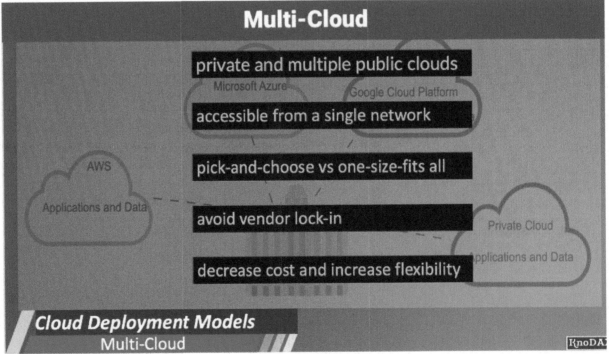

Figure 3.14 multi-cloud

Cloud Computing and AWS Introduction

A multi-cloud model use case generally fits into a larger organization, where one department cloud needs, and budgets may not be aligned with the other departments. For example, the engineering department needs cloud resources for their development and deployment needs. However, the marketing and HR departments cannot use the cloud setup or resources of the engineering department because marketing and HR departments may have additional requirements.

In these scenarios, organizations sometimes choose from the available public cloud providers that best fit their computing and budget needs rather than using the one-size-fits-all solution. Because of utilizations of multi-cloud providers, organizations not only avoid their dependency on a single provider, but multi-cloud also can help them decrease cost and increase flexibility in the long run.

Multitenancy

What is Multitenancy?

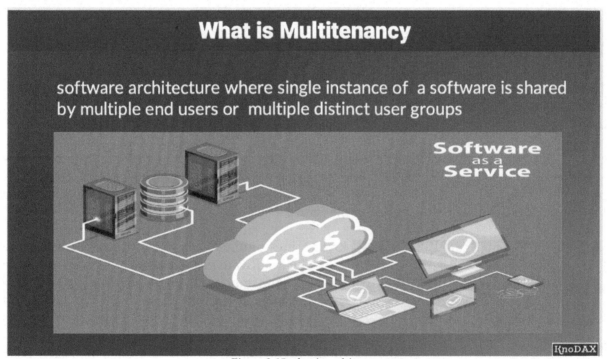

Figure 3.15 what is multitenancy

Multitenancy is a software architecture where an instance of a single software can be used by multiple end-users or multiple distinct user groups.

SaaS software, such as Salesforce, Google Gmail, Microsoft Office 365, TurboTax are typical examples of multi-tenancy.

Figure 3.16 multitenant software examples

Single Tenancy

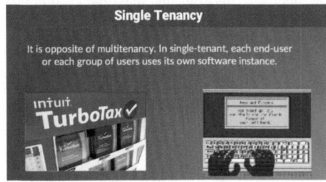

Figure 3.17 single tenancy

As the name suggests, it is the opposite of multitenancy. In a single tenant, each end-user or each group of users uses its software instance. There are plenty of examples. Let's take an example of tax software, for instance, TurboTax software has its SaaS version. They also have their old classic desktop version, which you can buy and install and use as a single user or single tenant. The typing software can be another example. There are many SaaS software to practice typing, but you can also purchase a single-tenant desktop version of typing software.

Journey to SaaS from Timesharing

The multitenancy concept is not new. In the mainframe era, which was around the 1960s. At that time to share mainframe computing resources among multiple users, timeshare software was used.

Cloud computing now uses the same multitenancy idea to allow sharing of computing resources – particularly in the public cloud computing deployment model. The pool of computing resources – processing power and memory – is divided among multiple users or multitenant in the public cloud. This multitenancy is at the server level.

Figure 3.18 journey to SaaS from timesharing

SaaS brings multitenancy to the software architecture – in which software instance is shared among multiple users. An important point to note is that like multitenancy in mainframe, or like in public cloud computing, in SaaS, data for each user is also separated or isolated, even though the same software instance is shared. To separate data, typically, SaaS providers separate databases for each SaaS client.

Multitenancy Advantages

Multitenancy saves cost and enables flexibility. With respect to saving cost advantage, the reason is apparent. Since the computing resources are consolidated and shared among multiple users or clients, this sharing helps keep costs lower for individual users in a multitenant environment.

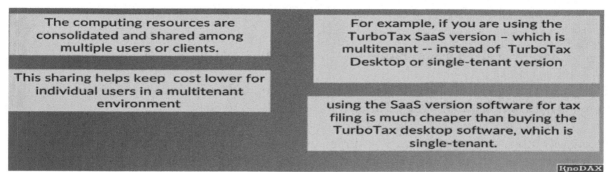

Figure 3.19 multitenancy advantage - cost savings

For example, if you are using the TurboTax SaaS version, instead of TurboTax Desktop or single-tenant version, using the SaaS version software for tax filing is much cheaper than buying the TurboTax desktop single-tenant software.

Another advantage of multitenancy is that it enables flexibility. As we know, doing estimation is a challenging exercise. If you over-provision, the cost will go high. On the other hand, if you under-provision, then your output would suffer.

Figure 3.20 multitenancy advantage - enables flexibility

But in a multitenant environment, you only pay for what you use. Also, you would be free to manage the resources such as applying a patch, securing as the provider takes care of resource management.

Cloud Computing Deployment Models Summary

To summarize, there are four types of cloud deployment models: **public cloud, private cloud, hybrid cloud, and community cloud**. Each has its own pros & cons based on the organizations computing needs.

Public clouds are prevalent and commonly used; however, organizations with tighter security and regulatory needs prefer private clouds. The hybrid model utilizes the best of both private and public clouds. Community clouds save cost for organizations willing to collaborate and share; however, it is generally not commonly used. The multi-cloud model avoids dependency on a single cloud vendor, provides lots of flexibility, and it is versatile. It combines private, public, and many types of public cloud providers.

Related YouTube Videos

Cloud Computing Deployment Models:
https://youtu.be/FAOSS8A9-Rg Mulitenancy: https://youtu.be/-_yJjAmVlXU

Chapter Review Questions

For the questions given below, please mark them if they are true or false.

1. A public cloud, in general, has a limited amount of computing resources and storage available, and it is not easily scalable. True / False

2. Organizations with solid security and regulatory requirements such as banks and healthcare providers prefer private cloud – particularly total on-premises cloud solutions. True / False

3. In a hybrid cloud, there is integration involved between private and public cloud. This can cause potential performance issues because of network latency and security risks as data are shared between public and private clouds. True / False

4. The multi-cloud model use case generally fits into a larger organization, where one department's cloud needs, and budgets may not be aligned with the other departments. True / False

5. Multitenancy is a software architecture where an instance of a single software can be used by multiple end-users or multiple distinct user groups. True / False

6. Multitenancy is a feature of cloud computing platform, which enables more than user to access the software deployed on the cloud concurrently. True / False

Please select the correct answer from the given choices for the questions below.

7. Which one is the best scenario for the public cloud deployment model?

    a. An organization that has highly sensitive information about users
    b. Applications computing needs are constant -- the same number of users and the same use cases.
    c. The organization has to constantly deal with scalability issues -- as the load on the system is unpredictable.
    d. The organization has underutilized computing resources.

8. Which of the following options is the best use case of a private cloud?

    a. The organization doesn't need to be concerned about data control. There is no legal or regulatory requirement of where data should data be kept. With regards to the load, the overall load on the system is fairly consistent.
    b. The organization needs to have maximum control over its data as data is of a highly sensitive type. With regards to the load, the overall load on the system is extremely unpredictable and the organization doesn't have the IT infrastructure capacity to manage unpredictable compute resource requirements.
    c. The organization doesn't care where data is stored as data is not of a sensitive type. With regards to the load, the overall load patten on the system is fairly constant.

d. The organization development teams are involved in many short-term projects and sometimes demand computing resources are unpredictable but manageable with its internal IT infrastructure.

9. Which of following options is the best use case for using a hybrid cloud?

a. An organization that has a fairly large IT infrastructure and there are no regulatory requirements. Additionally, the organization doesn't have any sensitive data and applications.
b. An organization that has sensitive data and applications along with regulatory requirements. However, the organization needs additional computing and storage resources for non-critical dev and test applications to save costs on IT infrastructure.
c. An organization whose IT infrastructure is under-utilized and on average the load is consistent. d. A start-up that is developing its product needs servers for dev and test environment only, but the demand for computing resources are unpredictable. The production date is yet decided as the company is in a highly competitive domain. That's the company management is very careful in releasing the product.

10. Which of the following options is the best selection choice with regards to cloud computing security?

a. A private cloud is a better option if you need tight control over sensitive data.
b. Cloud computing is not for multitenant applications.
c. It doesn't matter if you choose public or private cloud with regards to the security of data.
d. A community cloud is more secure than a private cloud.

11. Which of the following cloud deployment models is the best characterization of AWS?

a. Public
b. Private
c. Hybrid
d. Community

12. Which of the following SaaS software is a multi-tenant type?

a. Microsoft Office 365
b. Facebook
c. Gmail
d. all of them

13. Cloud computing environments can be of both types either multi-tenant or single-tenant -- though the multi-tenant type of cloud computing environment is more common. Which of the following options is an advantage of a multi-tenant cloud computing environment over a single-tenant cloud computing environment?

a. enhanced data security

b. faster performance
c. cost savings
d. all of them

Chapter 4. Cloud Applications Deployment Models

"The cloud services companies of all sizes...The cloud is for everyone. The cloud is a democracy." --Marc Benioff, Founder, CEO and Chairman, Salesforce

Digital transformation or modernization is challenging, and for many organizations that already have their applications in a non-cloud environment, it could take a year or many years of effort to complete modernization. The success of modernization or cloud migration depends on many factors. The first is deciding which deployment model is the right choice for the applications.

When deploying applications on the cloud, we have mainly two approaches: one is all-in, and the other is hybrid. And there is another choice, which is on-premises, in which all IT infrastructure and IT assets are deployed on an on-premises data center as a private cloud.

All-In Deployment Model

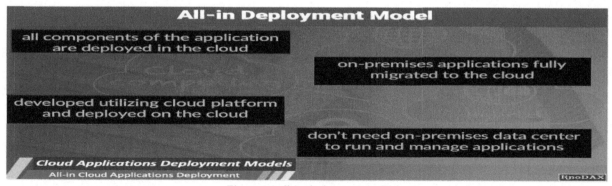

Figure 4.1 all-in deployment model

In an all-in deployment model, all components of applications are deployed in the cloud. In this deployment model, either application is directly developed utilizing cloud components and deployed on the cloud – also can be called "cloud native" deployment. Or earlier deployed applications on the on-premises data center have been migrated entirely to the cloud – which is "all in with cloud" deployment.

Hybrid Deployment Model

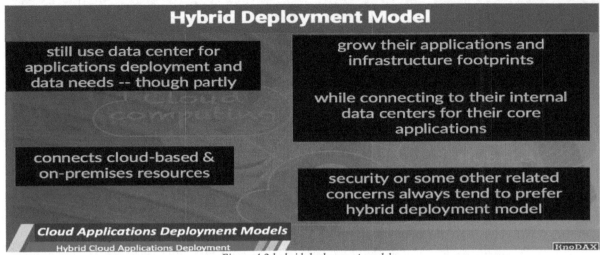

Figure 4.2 hybrid deployment model

In a hybrid deployment model (or hybrid model), as the name says in this deployment model, we still use an on-prem data center for applications deployment and data needs, though partly – means applications are not entirely moved or migrated on the cloud.

In a hybrid model, cloud-based resources are connected with the existing on-prem data center resources. This is a standard method of the hybrid model where organizations grow their applications and infrastructure footprints on the cloud while connecting to their internal data centers for their core applications.

Because of security or other related concerns, organizations in some domains always prefer a hybrid deployment model.

On-premises

Though cloud computing main advantages come from a public cloud, organizations in banking, finance, and health care domains have solid regulations and other strong security requirements compared to other business domains. Because of these and other reasons, such as if the cost-benefit analysis is not making a much difference to pivot to complete public or hybrid, they prefer complete on-premises private cloud deployment.

Related YouTube Video
Cloud Applications Deployment Models: https://youtu.be/-XOb_-g57XY

Chapter Review Questions

For the questions given below, please mark them if they are true or false.

1. Because of security or other related concerns, organizations in some domains always prefer a hybrid deployment model. True / False

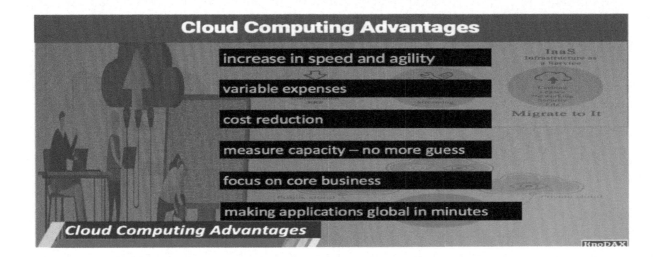

Chapter 5. Cloud Computing Advantages

"If someone asks me what cloud computing is, I try not to get bogged down with definitions. I tell them that, simply put, cloud computing is a better way to run your business." -- Marc Benioff, Founder, CEO and Chairman, Salesforce

Well, there is no point learning something if we don't have reasoning for "why?" That being the case, in this chapter, we will learn about the advantages of cloud computing. That way, we can reason why organizations need to adopt cloud computing.

One of the advantages of cloud computing is an increase in speed and agility. The other is variable expense instead of upfront cost, which we usually encounter in the classical, traditional computing model. The next advantage is cost reduction. Another advantage is measuring what and how much IT resources we need instead of guessing. Furthermore, since IT resources are much easier to procure and manage in cloud computing, we can focus on the core business. Another advantage is deploying applications to global customers in a few minutes. This is a valuable advantage as globally deploying applications is a bit time-consuming in a non-cloud environment. In this chapter, one by one, we will discuss these main advantages of cloud computing.

Increase in Speed and Agility

In a cloud computing environment, provisioning resources are just one or a few clicks away. This ease of provisioning resources provides a huge advantage in domains where request fluctuations vary heavily. Since the capacity of the machines

Figure 5.0.1 increase in speed and agility

can be scaled up and down easily, cloud computing becomes a practical solution choice in these domains or use cases.

Let's take a hypothetical example of CNN. In a non-cloud environment with no auto-scaling feature, if some significant newsworthy event happens, the CNN website or apps may suddenly notice a heavy increase in traffic, possibly resulting in degradation of service quality. Cloud computing can be leveraged in this situation. For example, CNN can scale up by launching more servers to meet the sudden increase in demand and then scale down when traffic comes to normal. Furthermore, services can be temporarily shut down if not required. Or, to save cost, they can be entirely terminated if they are not needed. As you can see that lots of options are there for saving operating technology infrastructure costs as well.

Let's take another hypothetical example to understand how cloud computing helps improve speed and agility. Suppose an organization needs resources as soon as possible to do some proof-of-concept (POC) type of work for some critical business requirements. They can tap into a cloud computing platform to get the resources quickly up and running. This helps organizations reduce the time. As the time it takes to make these resources available is reduced significantly, in many cases from weeks to within a few minutes.

Variable Expenses

Another advantage of cloud computing is a variable cost vs. upfront capital expenditure in the traditional style. In cloud computing, you avoid buying servers upfront – instead, you pay only for the services you use.

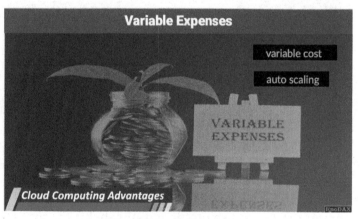

Figure 5.2 variable expenses

Let's consider this with a hypothetical example of an e-commerce company doing business for around 2000. The company would buy high-end servers to scale up to meet the significant increase in demand during Christmas time. But, when sales were not usually high, those expensive servers were not fully utilized and would remain idle for a while.

On the other hand, in the cloud computing platform, say AWS, using the auto-scaling service, new servers will be launched automatically (depending on configuration matrix such as CPU utilization, IO) when the load on the servers increases. And the servers will be terminated when the server load decreases -- you just need a few configurations. And the result is massive savings in cost.

You can see the point. Depending on how big the e-commerce organization is for its technology infrastructure, the cost-benefit would be significant if that eCommerce organization was transitioned to a cloud computing platform.

Cost Reduction

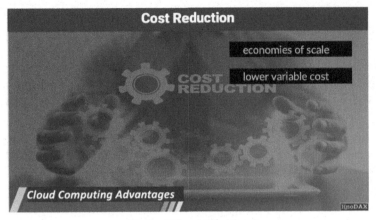

Figure 5.3 cost reduction

Next, let's talk about how cloud computing platform helps in reducing costs. Another advantage of cloud computing is that organizations can benefit hugely in price from massive economies of scale.

Cloud computing can achieve a lower variable cost than we would get on our own by buying individual servers or setting up VM, etc. Because thousands of customers use the cloud, cloud providers, for example, AWS, Google, Microsoft can provide cloud services at lower prices.

Measure Capacity – No More Guess

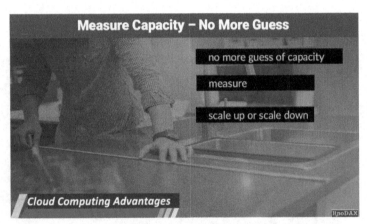

Figure 5.4 measure capacity -- no more guess

Another advantage is no more guesstimate of capacity. Usually, when we make the capacity decision for servers to deploy applications, there is a higher likelihood of getting expensive servers, which may be sitting idle most of the time. Or we end up having resources that would be very limited in capacity.

In other words, it's challenging to do capacity estimations -- which is true though in some cases. For capacity estimations, we can use cloud computing -- no need to do guesstimate for the infrastructure in cloud computing. With a cloud computing model, we can measure how much capacity we require, and then within a few minutes, resources can be scaled up or scaled down as the requirements change.

Focus on Business

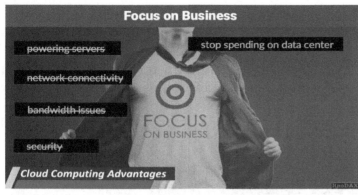

Figure 5.5 focus on business

Another advantage to talk about is that organizations can focus on their core business when using cloud computing platforms.

Cloud computing helps organizations focus on their core business instead of powering their servers, network connectivity, bandwidth issues, security. And many other things they must deal with if organizations have their technology infrastructure in an on-prem data center. By transitioning to the cloud computing platform, organizations can change direction and stop spending on running and maintaining their data centers. This allows organizations to focus on their core competencies in doing their business.

Applications Global in Minutes

And the last we have here is making applications available globally. Another advantage of cloud computing is the ability to make applications available worldwide within a few minutes.

Figure 5.6 applications global in minutes

Organizations can now quickly deploy their applications to multiple locations around the world with just a few clicks. This allows organizations to provide redundancy across the globe and reduce the application's latency.

Having redundant deployment across the globe helps increase applications availability. In addition, reducing network latency helps improve applications' network performance. The availability and reduced network latency translate the organization's customers' footprint and applications' degree of usability. And the critical point is that the organizations using cloud computing get these at a minimal cost and time.

There is one important point to bring to attention, which is the level playing field. Going global was very expensive in terms of cost and process. Only the organizations having deep pockets could afford to do. But cloud computing makes the deployment of applications globally – a level playing field. With cloud computing, any organization can deploy its applications globally at minimal cost and time.

Summary

In summary, cloud computing has transformed technology infrastructure. It has impacted all types of organizations: traditional IT organizations such as banks, insurance, healthcare, or software engineering organizations in all sizes -- large, medium, small, or startups.

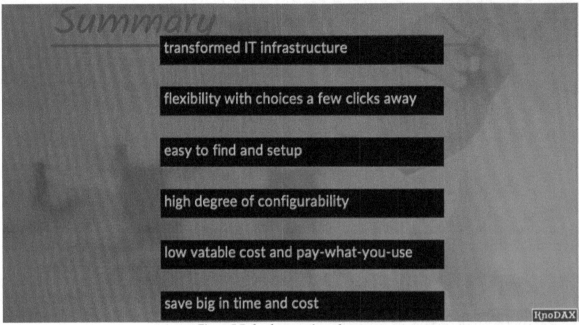

Figure 5.7 cloud computing advantages

And the reasons are apparent. First, cloud computing provides flexibility with so many choices a few clicks away. Second, cloud computing resources are easy to find and set up because of the high flexibility in making changes just by changing configurations. Third, we have excellent cost options: a low variable cost and pay-as-you-go pricing model. Over and above, nowadays, because of competition among cloud providers, there are choices of various pricing options. These pricing options could potentially help save big in cost for how organizations used to get IT infrastructure resources traditionally. And finally, cloud computing saves time as getting readily available all kinds of resources are very fast and easy, and deploying applications to global users is much quicker, thus saving time in this effort.

Related YouTube Video
Cloud Computing Advantages: https://youtu.be/pg1vKL7Xiyw

Chapter Review Questions

Please select the correct answer from the given choices for the questions below.

1. Which of the following options is the advantage of cloud computing?

a. increase in speed and agility
b. variable expenses
c. focus on core business
d. all of them

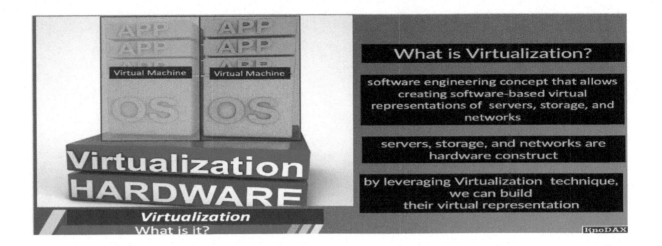

Chapter 6. Virtualization, Virtual Machine, and Hypervisor

"done on IBM mainframes in the 1960s, but Gerald J. Popek and Robert P. Goldberg codified the framework that describes the requirements for a computer system to support virtualization. Their 1974 article "Formal Requirements for Virtualizable Third Generation Architectures" describes the roles and properties of virtual machines and virtual machine monitors that we still use today."

— Matthew Portnoy, Virtualization Essentials

"Divide-and-Conquer" is one of the fundamental tenets in computer science, and we see examples of this principle in solving many types of software solutions. That is being said -- we can divide a single process into multiple execution paths, called multithreading. Likewise, on an operating system, we can run multiple processes, which is called multiprocessing. In other words, we can run multiple execution paths inside a single process and multiple processes on an operating system. On a similar token, the question is: can we run more than one operating system on single physical hardware? The answer is yes -- we can. Virtualization is the software engineering mechanism, which allows running multiple operating systems on a single physical hardware. In this chapter, you will learn about virtualization, virtual machine (instance of an operating system), and hypervisor, which is a go-to system between an operating system and physical hardware.

Virtualization

What is Virtualization?

Virtualization essentially creates virtual computer systems. Virtualization, or in practical terms, virtual computer systems, allows organizations to run more than one operating system on a single server. As a result, virtualization helps in reducing physical servers needs.

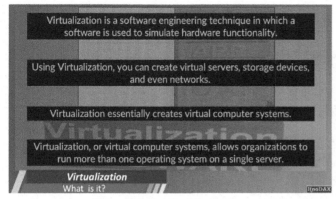

Figure 6.1 what is virtualization

As you can see, virtualization is a game-changer with respect to saving costs in buying and maintaining physical servers. Typically, we run one operating system on one server. However, in virtualization, since more than one operating system can be run on a single physical hardware, organizations can reduce their need to buy and maintain physical servers. The reason is virtualization helps them consolidate their servers' needs in fewer servers.

Why is Virtualization Needed?

Let's continue our discussion about virtualization further, imagine a scenario suppose we have a server that is being utilized minimally. Wouldn't it be better to utilize it in some way where we can use this server's resources to create another server inside that server? That's the basic idea behind virtualization.

Let's take another example. As we know, maintaining consistent SLA is very important in critical applications. How can we achieve consistent SLA when running multiple applications on the physical server? Maintaining consistent SLA would be a guessing game as each application would have to compete with other applications' processes for the resources. One way to handle this is to run each application in a separate

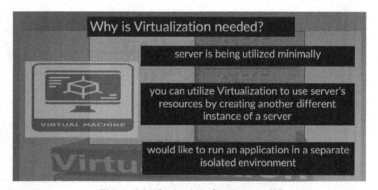

Figure 6.2 why is virtualization needed

isolated environment on the same physical server. That way, the application would not have to compete with other processes for the resources. This running applications in their different separate environment would help in providing consistent service level agreement (SLA). We can use the Virtualization technique to create a different independent running environment for each running application on the same physical server.

What Can be Virtualized?

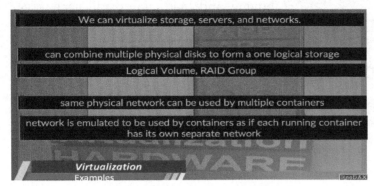

Let's talk about what we can virtualize. We can virtualize servers, storage, and networks. This means these hardware constructs can be created in software form as well using virtualization.

Figure 6.3 what can be virtualized

Using **Virtualization**, we can run multiple servers on the same physical server. These virtual servers are called virtual machines or VMs. We will about virtual machines later in the chapter. For example, we can run Windows and Linux operating systems as virtual machines as two entirely different environments on a single physical machine. Each VM would have its own RAM, storage, and network.

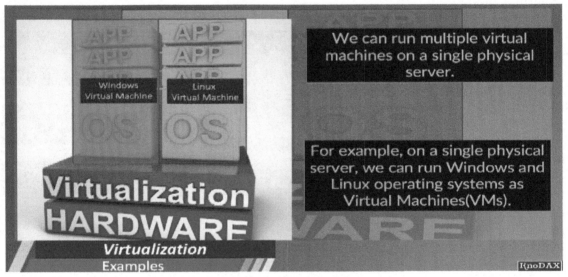

Figure 6.4 virtualization examples

Not only using **Virtualization**, we can run multiple separate operating systems on the same physical server, but also using **Virtualization** we can run multiple applications in a completely separated isolated environment on the same physical machine. This type of virtualization is called containerization, for example, Docker container. We will learn about Docker later in this book.

Besides server virtualization, using the Virtualization technique, storage can be virtualized as well. For example, multiple physical disks can be combined to form one logical storage (a form of virtual storage), which can be assigned to a server. Examples are Logical Volume, the RAID (Redundant Array of Independent/Inexpensive Disks) group.

In addition to server and storage virtualization, the network can also be virtualized using the Virtualization technique. Using network virtualization, a physical network can be used by multiple containers (separate runtime environment) running on the same physical server. The physical network is emulated in such a way so that it would be used by multiple containers as if each running container has its separate network.

Another type of virtualization is desktop virtualization. Desktop virtualization enables multiple desktop machines on a single physical server. This is also called desktop-as-a-server.

Virtualization Advantages

First, Virtualization increases the efficiency of servers by allowing resource usage optimization as opposed to underutilized servers. Since we can run multiple OS instances on the same physical server, we can efficiently utilize underutilized resources on that physical server.

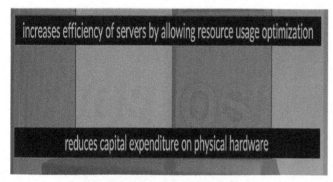

Figure 6.5 virtualization advantages

The next one is derived from the first one -- virtualization reduces capital expenditure on physical hardware. By using virtualization or virtual infrastructure we can consolidate many physical servers that are underutilized into a few servers. Thus, saving not only a physical server but also saving on space, power, air conditioning requirements, maintenance, and other things that go with having to have more servers instead of fewer servers to get the same operating functionality.

Virtual Machine

Figure 6.6 virtual machine

Now we got an understanding of Virtualization. As we talked about, one of the advantages of virtualization is that we can run multiple instances of operating systems -- also called virtual servers or VM – on single physical hardware. The virtualization technique used to create virtual servers, such as Windows or Linux servers, is called a virtual machine.

The virtual machine is also called virtual computer system, or VM, which is the more popular term for virtual machines.

We can think of a virtual machine or VM as a separate isolated container having its own operating system and applications. VMs are discrete, separate, and isolated, self-contained, and completely independent.

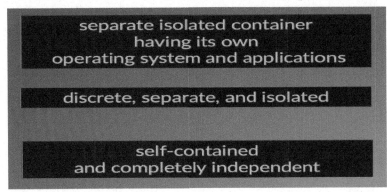

Figure 6.7 virtual machine features

Because they are self-contained and completely independent, we can launch multiple VMs on a single physical server. For example, we can have a Linux virtual machine and a Windows virtual machine, both of which can be run on a single physical server in their separate isolated environment. Not just two -- this is just an example. We can run many instances of operating systems on the same physical server. Having multiple VMs on single physical servers enables various operating systems and applications to run on one physical server. This physical server is also called **host** as it hosts multiple VMs.

Hypervisor

What is Hypervisor?

Figure 6.8 hypervisor

As we discussed, using virtualization, we can run multiple instances of operating systems on the same physical hardware. In other words, using virtualization, we can set up virtual machines. Now the question is: how do virtual machines -- as they run on the same physical hardware -- get the computing resources such as processors, memory, or storage?

There is a concept called Hypervisor or Virtual Machine Monitor, using which virtual machines get the computing resources such as processor, memory, or storage. The hypervisor is software that creates and manages virtual machines, and it also mediates communication between hosts and virtual machines.

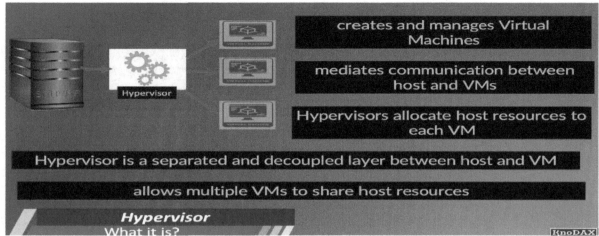

Figure 6.9 what is hypervisor

A hypervisor is a separate and decoupled layer between host and VM. The hypervisor allocates and shares host resources with each VM. In other words, a hypervisor allows multiple guest VMs to share host resources such as processor, memory, and storage of the physical machine. For example, when we install hypervisor software and set up multiple guest VMs on it, hypervisor software will take care of sharing host resources with each VM.

Hypervisor Types

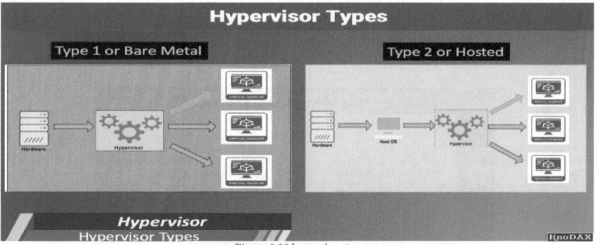

Figure 6.10 hypervisor types

There are two main types of hypervisors: one is referred to as Type 1 or Bare Metal Hypervisor. The other one is referred to as Type 2 or Hosted Hypervisor. A Type-1 hypervisor runs directly on top of bare metal hardware, acting as a lightweight OS. On the other hand, a Type-2 hypervisor runs on the OS. Since a Type-1 hypervisor runs straight on the hardware, it is also referred to as "Bare Metal," and a Type-2 hypervisor runs on the OS, that's why it is also called "Hosted."

Type-1 or Bare-Metal Hypervisor

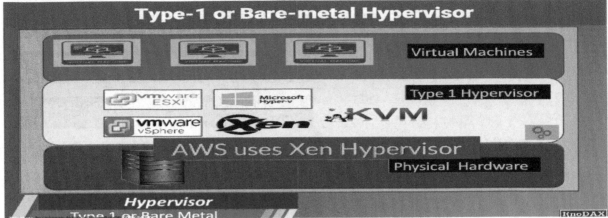

Figure 6.11 Type-1 or Bare-Metal Hypervisor

Let's talk further about Type-1 or Bare Metal hypervisor. It is installed directly on the hardware. In other words, Type-1 replaces the operating system. In place of the operating system, we install a Type-1 hypervisor.

Typically, a Type-1 or Bare Metal hypervisor is deployed most. There are some genuine reasons why this type of hypervisor is deployed most. Since it is directly installed on the hardware instead of on the OS, it is more secure than Type-2. And the other reason is that since no OS layer is involved, it performs better and more efficiently than Type-2 or hosted hypervisor. Because of security and performance reasons, Type-1 hypervisors are usually preferred for enterprises when deploying hypervisors on their data centers.

Type-2 or Hosted Hypervisor

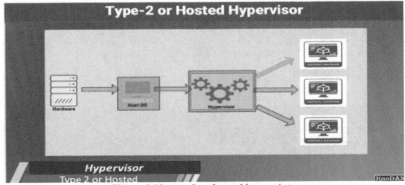

Figure 6.12 type-2 or hosted hypervisor

As you can see in the diagram, Type-2 or Hosted hypervisor runs on the host operating system.

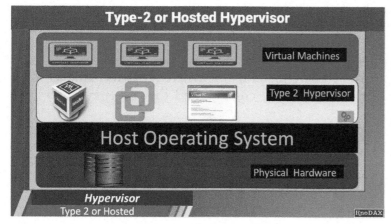

This is another diagram of a Type-2 hypervisor or Hosted hypervisor. In the diagram as you can see that at the bottom layer, we have the physical hardware, then the OS is installed. Since this is a Type-2 hypervisor diagram, first a hypervisor is installed on the OS, then virtual machines are installed. Examples of Type-2 hypervisors that run on host operating systems are Oracle Virtual Box, VMware Workstation, Microsoft Virtual PC.

Figure 6.13 type-2 or hosted hypervisor

The main difference between Type-1 and Type-2 is that Type-1 hypervisors are installed on bare metal and Type-2 hypervisors are installed on an operating system.

Related YouTube Video
Virtualization, VM, and Hypervisor: https://youtu.be/7CLytaxC3Lo

Chapter Review Questions

Exercise

1. Setup Linux Virtual Machine on Oracle Virtual Box and Install Apache Web Server on the Linux Virtual Machine.

Hint: Please follow the YouTube video: https://youtu.be/FODXLgAe2GQ to help in this exercise.

For the questions given below, please mark them if they are true or false.

2. Virtualization is a software engineering technique in which software is used to simulate hardware functionality. True / False

3. Virtual Machines are discrete, separated, isolated, self-contained, and completely independent. True / False

4. The hypervisor is software that creates and manages virtual machines, and it also mediates communication between hosts and Virtual machines. True / False

5. Type-1 Hypervisor performs better and more efficiently than Type-2 or Hosted Hypervisor because Type-1 Hypervisor is directly installed on the hardware instead of on the OS. True / False

Please select the correct answer from the given choices for the questions given below.

6. Which of the following options is the best selection choice with regards to the bare metal hypervisor?

    a. The bare metal hypervisor runs on top of a native operating system.
    b. The bare-metal hypervisor runs on a bare-metal that is where it has its name. Using a bare-metal hypervisor, virtual machines can be created, and the server resources are shared.
    c. The bare-metal hypervisor supports only one type of operating system.
    d. all of them

7. Which of the following types of hypervisors provides better performance?

    a. software based
    b. firmware based
    c. storage based
    d. none of them

8. In cloud computing, which of the following options is used to separate and assign physical resources such as memory and CPU?

    a. Load Balancer
    b. Switch
    c. BIOS
    d. Hypervisor

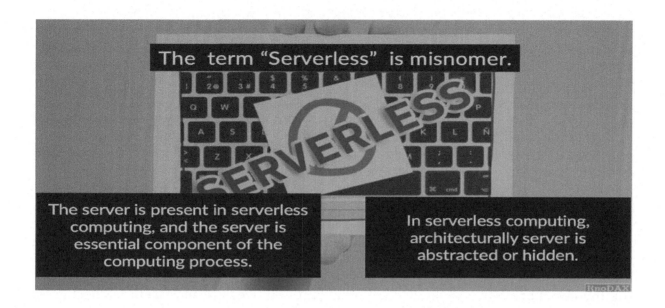

Chapter 7. Serverless Computing

In software engineering, abstraction is a powerful tool to hide what varies. Serverless computing is a modern computing paradigm primarily germinated from the power of abstraction. Serverless computing -- a modern cloud computing paradigm – is getting popular quickly. In this chapter, we will learn what serverless computing is, its features, use cases, pros & cons, and many other related aspects. Let's start with what serverless computing is.

What is Serverless Computing?

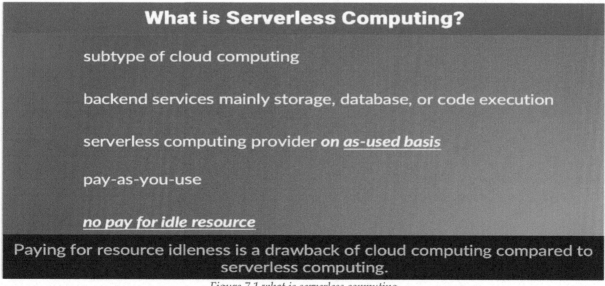

Figure 7.1 what is serverless computing

Serverless computing is a subtype of **cloud computing**. The interesting point to note is that word **serverless** in the term **serverless computing** is a misnomer; servers are an essential component of the computing process in serverless computing. In other words, the server or servers are used to process requests in a typical fashion – there is nothing special about serverless computing in the processing sense.

The question is then how it differs from regular computing. In serverless computing, we deal with an abstraction layer. In other words, we don't deal with or manage the server or operating system directly, which we would do in traditional computing or cloud computing. This abstraction layer sets up an illusion of serverless.

Let's understand that further. Suppose we have a use case to create a thumbnail image when an image is uploaded to a particular folder on the server. We develop a web service and deploy the code on the server, and the program is working fine – which means the web service is creating thumbnail images of the uploaded images.

This thumbnail processing application is working fine. But we have an issue that we get billed from the cloud provider for the instance even though the server is idle most of the time. The reason is that the average number of images processed each hour is around five (5 images/hour), and the processing time is 1 second. So, this is where we (as a software engineer) would need to think about a solution where we would pay only for the actual processing time, not for the idle time of the server.

And that's where serverless computing fits in. In serverless computing, servers are made available on-demand to process the request, and you would only be billed for the processing time. Serverless computing vendors have different cloud services, classifying them as **serverless computing** types. We will know about those services later in this chapter to get more clarity about **serverless computing.**

Serverless Computing Features

Automatic Provisioning of Computing Resources

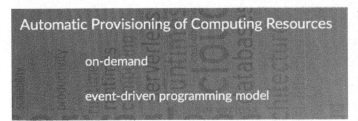

Serverless vendors automatically provision computing resources needed to run code both on-demand or in response to the trigger of an event in an event-driven programming model.

Figure 7.2 automatic provisioning of computing resources

Elastic Scalability

Not only does it automatically provision computing resources, but serverless computing also has the feature of elastic scalability. It means computing resources are scaled up to meet the demand of increased requests to maintain service level agreements (SLA) without degradation in performance to maintain quality output. Conversely, it scales down as the number of requests goes

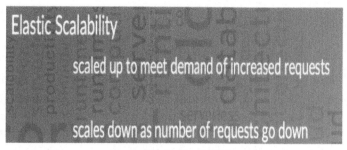

Figure 7.3 elastic scalability

down and shuts down completely when there is no request. The idea of elastic scalability saves costs, and it helps vendors efficiently utilize resources.

Faster Delivery Code

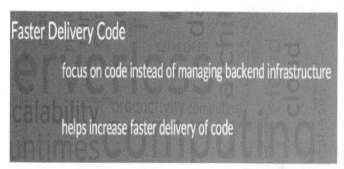

Figure 7.4 faster delivery of code

Another feature is productivity. To be more specific, it is about the faster delivery of code. In serverless architecture, engineers would have to focus on code instead of managing backend cloud infrastructure and tasks such as provisioning, scaling, patching, and other related things. As a result, serverless computing helps increase faster delivery of code. The serverless computing provider manages backend cloud infrastructure and operational tasks such as provisioning servers, scaling, patching.

Serverless Computing Backend Service Types

Mainly database, storage, function-as-a-service (FaaS) are the type of backend services in serverless computing. Serverless computing (serverless architecture) is well suited in event-driven and stream processing-related applications because these applications have some critical quality attributes to consider. These quality attributes are scalability and latency; the other is, at times, idleness (for example, an online store may not get any online order in some time duration) attributes.

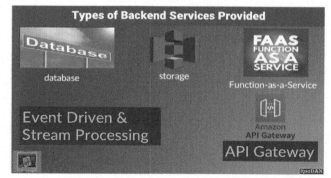

Figure 7.5 types of backend services provided

The other type of backend service in serverless computing is the API gateway. The API gateway manages (delegates) HTTP call to web services such as routing, rate limits, CORS, and authentication. Or in other words, API Gateway delegates HTTP requests to the code block implemented as function-as-a-service (FaaS). Essentially, these web services are wrappers over the FaaS code.

Serverless Computing Stack

We understood serverless computing and types of backend services that qualified as serverless computing. Now, let's know how we can combine and use these backend services -- which form a serverless computing stack -- to implement serverless computing use cases. An understanding serverless stack will help us rationalize how to combine different back-end services to design and build serverless architectural solutions. Serverless computing stack mainly includes function-as-a-service (FaaS), database and storage, event-driven & stream processing, and API gateway. We will look at each of them in this section.

Function-as-a-Service (FaaS)

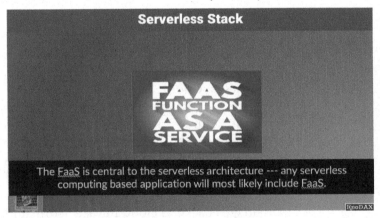

Figure 7.6 serverless computing stack: FaaS

The function-as-a-service (FaaS) is central to the serverless architecture. FaaS, which is central to the serverless architecture, deals with the application code in the serverless stack. Therefore, any serverless computing-based application will most likely include FaaS.

To understand function-as-a-service from the serverless stack, let's look into the diagram shown below. Let's assume in this diagram that the web application shown in the diagram is implemented using serverless architecture.

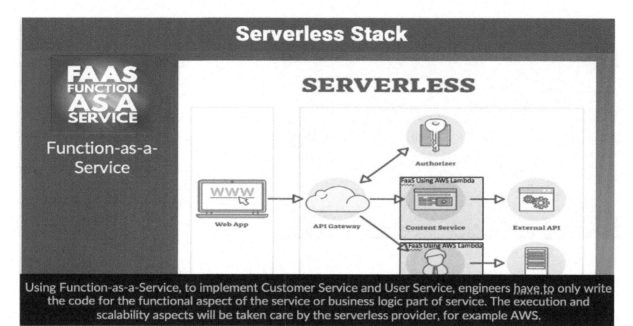

Figure 7.7 serverless stack – FaaS use case example

Let's focus on Customer Service and User Service. Customer Service is interacting with an external API. User Service is interacting with an external database for the user information, for example, user verification and new user registration. In this use case, since Customer and User services are not called very less (let's assume five requests/hour), we can leverage function-as-a-service, for example, AWS Lambda, from the serverless stack if you use the AWS cloud platform. That way, we would only pay for the processing time of serverless services instead of running a server that would be sitting idle most of the time.

Function-as-a-service (FaaS) of serverless computing is a massive plus if you look at it from the timesaving and productivity perspective. Using function-as-a-service, we would have to write only code for the functional aspect of the service or business logic part of the service, for example, to implement Customer Service and User Service. The execution and scalability aspects of the application will be taken care of by the serverless provider, for example, AWS.

Database and Storage

Let's look into other components of a serverless stack. In most enterprise-grade applications, database and storage are the foundation. We usually run a database instance (or storage such as AWS S3 commonly used in cloud-based data engineering applications) or instances on a separate server and build an abstraction layer to connect to the database. This abstraction layer is called Data Layer or Database Layer.

When applying serverless architecture, for the database and storage, instead of previsioning

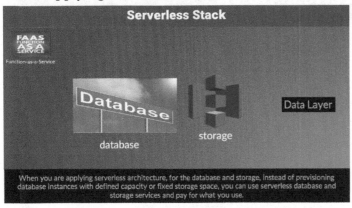

database instances with defined capacity or fixed storage space, we can use serverless database and storage services and pay for what we use. Additionally, serverless database and storage services will scale automatically. For example, using serverless architecture, User Service can store user registration in the serverless database such as DynamoDB or Amazon Arora to optimize the cost and scalability of User Service.

Figure 7.8 serverless stack -- database & storage

Event-Driven & Stream Processing

Another type of component in the serverless stack is event-driven and stream processing. If your application is event-driven or a stream processing application, you could use serverless architecture.

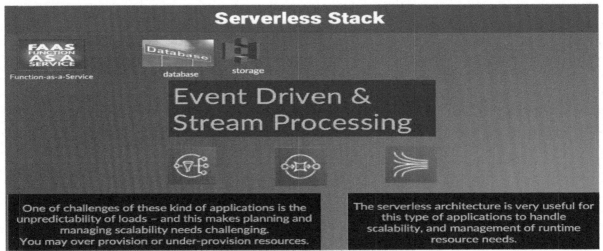

Figure 7.9 serverless stack -- event driven & stream processing

One of the challenges of these applications is the unpredictability of loads, which makes planning and managing scalability needs challenging. As a result, you may over-provision or under-provision resources. The serverless architecture is beneficial for these applications to handle scalability and manage runtime resource needs. AWS has many serverless services for event-driven and stream processing applications. For example, AWS SNS (Simple Notification Service), AWS SQS (Simple Queue Service), AWS Kinesis are some examples of serverless services.

API Gateway

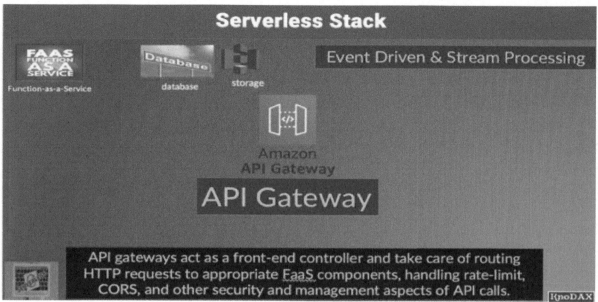

Figure 7.10 serverless stack -- API gateway

API gateways are another serverless architectural component. API gateways act as a front-end controller and take care of routing HTTP requests to appropriate FaaS components. Additionally, API gateways can handle rate limits, CORS, and other security and management aspects of API calls.

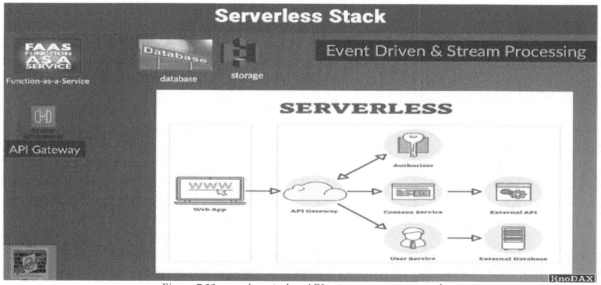

Figure 7.11 serverless stack -- API gateway use case example

Coming back to this architecture diagram of User Management which we are looking into. The API gateway component in the diagram, as shown above, is a serverless component that handles the authentication of a user and other API management-related aspects. Imagine building the API gateway in a non-serverless way – as you can imagine, handling scalability will become a challenging engineering exercise.

AWS Serverless Services

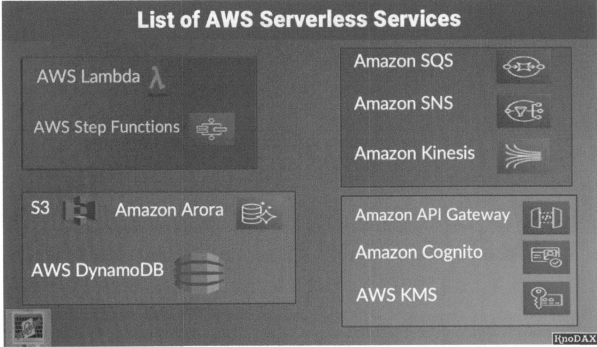

Figure 7.12 AWS serverless services

Since AWS is a cloud provider and provides backend services for serverless computing. Let's discuss AWS backend services of serverless type.

In the code execution category, AWS provides AWS Lambda and AWS Step Functions. AWS Lambda is a fully FaaS type of serverless service, which is used to write code. For example, we can write AWS Lambda code in Java, Python, or Node.js and in many other languages to implement business functions.

AWS Step Functions is a visual workflow service that helps build serverless applications by orchestrating AWS services to automate business processes.

In the database and storage category, AWS has S3 (Simple Storage Service), Amazon Arora, and DynamoDB. Amazon Arora is a relational database service, and DynamoDB is a NoSQL service. These are all serverless services.

In event-driven and stream processing backend services, AWS has SQS (Simple Queue Service), SNS (Simple Notification Service), and Kinesis. SQS is AWS queuing service, SNS is a notification service, and Kinesis is a streaming service. Functionally, Kinesis is like Kafka.

The other services are Amazon API Gateway, Amazon Cognito. Amazon Cognito provides authentication, authorization, and user management-related functionalities to web and mobile applications. In addition, AWS KMS is an essential management service for encryption/decryption.

These are a few examples of AWS serverless services to give you an overview of serverless services from a serverless provider perspective.

Serverless Computing: Pros & Cons

Pros

The first is about cost. In general, serverless computing is a cost-effective solution for many application types—particularly web applications with an unpredictable number of requests. In a traditional cloud, we end up paying for the entire server resource, in which we may be paying for the unused or idle resources. But in serverless computing, we don't pay for idle resources.

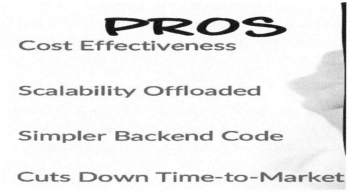

Next is scalability. Scalability is one of the main advantages of serverless computing. In serverless computing, engineers would not have to give much thought to scalability. We must design code to be scalable and stateless, though. And the serverless vendor would take care of making sure the system doesn't degrade as load increases.

Figure 7.13 serverless computing -- pros

Next on the list here is simpler backend code. As we know that function-as-a-service is one of the significant components of serverless architecture. Using FaaS, we can write highly cohesive code – implementing one and only one functional aspect. Since non-functional concerns are offloaded, this offloading simplifies the FaaS code.

And the last one we have is reduced time-to-market. Serverless architecture cuts down the significant time to market. Instead of planning and setting up servers for dev, test, and production, we can leverage serverless offerings from serverless providers -- thus saving huge in time.

You may wonder whether serverless computing doesn't have any drawbacks – yes, there are a few.

Cons

Let's talk about the cons of serverless before completing this topic – which is mainly latency in start-up and monitoring, debugging.

Since to run FaaS optimally, the server must be running. However, if the server or container is not processing, the provider shuts down the server or container to save energy and

Figure 7.14 serverless computing -- cons

computing resources. That being the case, when the subsequent request comes, the container needs to be started fresh – this start-up adds latency. The latency might be an issue if the load has lots of lags. However, if the requests are continuous, the restart will not be an issue. Serverless doesn't provide much cost savings for consistent or predictable workloads. However, it offers excellent protection for a sudden spike or unpredictable load patterns.

Another issue with serverless computing is related to monitoring and debugging. Monitoring and debugging is generally challenging in a distributed environment. For example, low-level debugging is tedious, mainly because of the abstraction of distributed cloud computing.

Serverless Computing: Use Cases

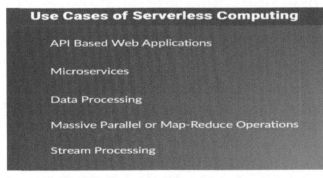

Figure 7.15 serverless computing -- use cases

The first typical use case is API-based applications. For example, suppose we have a web application that has APIs driven backend. Here, we can use FaaS to write functional code for APIs that interact with the database, and we can front the FaaS code with an API gateway. Typically, in API-based web applications on the cloud, we can leverage serverless if the load is unpredictable or there is a chance of a sudden spike in load.

The following use case is about microservices. As we notice, nowadays, many microservices applications are built using containers. However, using serverless can be an advantage with a fast turnaround as we can write highly cohesive code using FaaS to implement microservices.

Another potential use case is related to ETL type of applications. Serverless computing is a good solution for ETL projects such as data cleaning, transformation, enrichment, and validation because of unpredictable data requirements. Building a real-time ETL application on the same token and a related concept is also a good use case for serverless. We can leverage FaaS to write code for enrichment, validation, cleaning, and orchestration. Applications inherently parallel in computation, such as map-reduce type of applications, are also a good use case for serverless computing.

Summary

The serverless architecture stack provides a function-as-a-service component to write services without thinking about scalability issues. For example, it includes database and storage services without going through how many extra servers we need to handle additional loads. The serverless provider will take care of provisioning and scalability needs. And we only pay for the usage.

It provides services for event-driven and stream processing. However, in the non-serverless environment, we need to monitor and troubleshoot issues continuously and handle scalability issues. Therefore, there is always a possibility of over-provisioning or under-provisioning.

However, if you have worked on an event-driven or stream processing application in a non-serverless environment, you can easily understand how helpful serverless architecture is. We just focus on writing code for business logic or functional requirements and let serverless providers provide and manage runtime computing resources. Finally, we have an API gateway that fronts it with all kinds of things, such as request routing, rate limit, CORS, authentication, and many.

Related YouTube Video
Serverless Computing: https://youtu.be/zUyamR5iBms

Chapter Review Questions

For the questions given below, please mark them if they are true or false.

1. The term "Serverless" in "Serverless Computing" is a misnomer. The server is present in serverless computing, and the server is an essential component of the computing process. True / False

2. The serverless vendor provides backend services such as storage, database, or code execution on an as-used basis, and the payment model is pay-as-you-use. True / False

3. Serverless vendors automatically provision computing resources needed to run code both on-demand or in response to the trigger of an event in an event-driven programming model. True / False

4. Which is not a type of backend service provided in serverless computing? True / False

5. The FaaS is central to the serverless architecture. Therefore, any serverless computing-based application will most likely include FaaS. True / False 6. In the traditional cloud, you end up paying for the entire server resource, in which you may be paying for the unused or idle resources. But in serverless computing, you don't pay for idle resources. True / False
6. Scalability is one of the main advantages of serverless computing. Serverless vendors take care of making sure your system doesn't degrade as the load increases. True / False

Chapter 8. Docker Introduction

"Docker allows you to package an application with all of its dependencies into a standardized unit for software development." – **Docker**, *What is Docker*

The basic concept behind Docker is to run an application -- and all its dependencies -- completely isolated as if -- only your application -- is running on a server.

Moreover, the process of deploying and running an application should be repeatable. Therefore, an image -- to achieve this concept -- is used. This image contains all the source code and dependencies. This image is run each time the application needs to be run. As you go through the document further, this concept will become clear. The rest of the Docker is all about running commands for DevOps type of work. I have written this chapter from a simplistic viewpoint.

What is Docker?

Docker is virtualization technology. The Docker like virtual machines not only allows you to run applications in a different environment, but it does more. It is one of the critical DevOps technologies.

Using Docker, we can package application source code, including operating system libraries and all dependencies required to run the application into a Docker image. The Docker image can run in any Docker environment. The runtime environment of the Docker image is called a Docker container. Docker uses resource isolation – like how processes are isolated -- in the operating system kernel to run multiple containers on the same operating system.

Docker Overview from DevOps Perspective

Docker is one of the most valuable tools from the DevOps and automation perspective. So, let's try to understand Docker from the DevOps perspective.

Installation of Docker

First, we need to install Docker on the local system. The installation and how to configure the local Docker environment vary from platform to platform. However, once the Docker system is installed, the rest of all the operations and commands are the same irrespective of the operating system.

The Docker Desktop is a helpful tool for running and managing the local Docker environment. It is available for Windows and macOS. In this document, I'm using Docker Desktop for the Mac.

How to install Docker on Mac: https://docs.docker.com/desktop/mac/install/

How to install Docker on Windows: https://docs.docker.com/desktop/windows/install/

To understand this document, please make sure that Docker Desktop is installed so that you can also try out the commands mentioned in this document. Once the Docker is installed, and we are ready to roll our sleeves to learn Docker.

Use Case

Suppose you have a use case to set up a test environment of Apache Web Server on your local machine using Docker for POC (proof of concept) type of work.

Docker Image

In Docker, we start from a Docker image. Either we build a Docker image or pull (it is a Docker term) the already pre-built Docker image from a Docker registry. The Docker registry stores Docker images. For example, Docker Hub, Artifactory can be used as a Docker registry.

Docker Hub

The default Docker registry is Docker Hub. In our use case, we can get the Apache Web Server Docker image from the Docker Hub. To find out if an Apache Web Server Docker image is available on the Docker Hub. Let's visit dockerHub.com and search for "Apache Web Server."

As you can notice on the screenshot, the httpd image is listed in the search result. We will use this httpd image as this is an official image of the Apache HTTP Server.

Figure 8.1 docker hub

Once we have found our image, the next step is pulling the image on the local Docker system.

Pull Docker Image

To pull a Docker image, the command to use is docker pull. First, let's open a terminal to pull the Docker image. You will get many Docker commands if you just type 'docker' and press <return>. We have added screenshots of the output.

```
sksingh:~$ docker

Usage:  docker [OPTIONS] COMMAND

A self-sufficient runtime for containers

Options:
      --config string      Location of client config files (default "/Users/sksingh/.docker")
  -c, --context string     Name of the context to use to connect to the daemon (overrides
                           DOCKER_HOST env var and default context set with "docker context use")
  -D, --debug              Enable debug mode
  -H, --host list          Daemon socket(s) to connect to
  -l, --log-level string   Set the logging level ("debug"|"info"|"warn"|"error"|"fatal")
                           (default "info")
      --tls                Use TLS; implied by --tlsverify
      --tlscacert string   Trust certs signed only by this CA (default
                           "/Users/sksingh/.docker/ca.pem")
      --tlscert string     Path to TLS certificate file (default
                           "/Users/sksingh/.docker/cert.pem")
      --tlskey string      Path to TLS key file (default "/Users/sksingh/.docker/key.pem")
      --tlsverify          Use TLS and verify the remote
  -v, --version            Print version information and quit

Management Commands:
  builder     Manage builds
  config      Manage Docker configs
```

Figure 8.2 docker command help

```
    logs          Fetch the logs of a container
    pause         Pause all processes within one or more container
    port          List port mappings or a specific mapping for
    ps            List containers                                    docker pull
    pull          Pull an image or a repository from a registry
    push          Push an image or a repository to a registry
    rename        Rename a container
    restart       Restart one or more containers
    rm            Remove one or more containers
    rmi           Remove one or more images
    run           Run a command in a new container
    save          Save one or more images to a tar archive (streamed to STDOUT by default)
    search        Search the Docker Hub for images
    start         Start one or more stopped containers
    stats         Display a live stream of container(s) resource usage statistics
    stop          Stop one or more running containers
    tag           Create a tag TARGET_IMAGE that refers to SOURCE_IMAGE
    top           Display the running processes of a container
    unpause       Unpause all processes within one or more containers
    update        Update configuration of one or more containers
    version       Show the Docker version information
    wait          Block until one or more containers stop, then print their exit codes

Run 'docker COMMAND --help' for more information on a command.

To get more help with docker, check out our guides at https://docs.docker.com/go/guides/
sksingh:~$ clear
sksingh:~$ docker

Usage:  docker [OPTIONS] COMMAND

A self-sufficient runtime for containers

Options:
```

Figure 8.3 docker pull command

As you can see, we have highlighted the pull command, which we will use to pull the httpd Docker image from the Docker Hub.

Let's run "*docker pull <image name>*" command. In our case <image name> is "httpd" since we are pulling httpd image from Docker Hub.

```
sksingh:~$ docker pull httpd
Using default tag: latest
latest: Pulling from library/httpd
b380bbd43752: Pull complete
d0c6942edac3: Pull complete
d027638c026c: Pull complete
17082a2122d5: Pull complete
0b7d42e498cc: Pull complete
Digest: sha256:f03a63735d3653045a3b1f5490367415e9534d8abfe0b21252454dc85ca09800
Status: Downloaded newer image for httpd:latest
docker.io/library/httpd:latest
sksingh:~$ █
```

Figure 8.4 docker pull example

The httpd image is pulled from Docker Hub.

List Docker Image

How can we list the pulled image in our Docker environment? The command to list docker images: "*docker image ls*"

```
sksingh:~/myDockerDemo$ docker image ls
REPOSITORY     TAG        IMAGE ID        CREATED            SIZE
my-apache      latest     a7b36ec37dea    About a minute ago  138MB
httpd          2.4        d54056386fbb    6 days ago          138MB
sksingh:~/myDockerDemo$
```

Figure 8.5 docker command: docker image ls

Also, to list all the images, there is a command "*docker images -a*."

```
sksingh:~$ docker images -a
REPOSITORY     TAG        IMAGE ID        CREATED       SIZE
httpd          latest     d54056386fbb    5 days ago    138MB
sksingh:~$
```

Figure 8.6 docker command: docker images -a

As you can notice in the screenshot, the pulled httpd image is listed in my local Docker environment. We will discuss building our own Docker image and publish it to Docker Hub later in this document.

Run Docker Image

Let's run this pulled httpd Docker image. The Docker command to run a Docker image is:

```
$ docker run [OPTIONS] IMAGE [COMMAND] [ARG...]
```

With that, let's look into httpd image documentation on how to run this image on the Docker Hub.

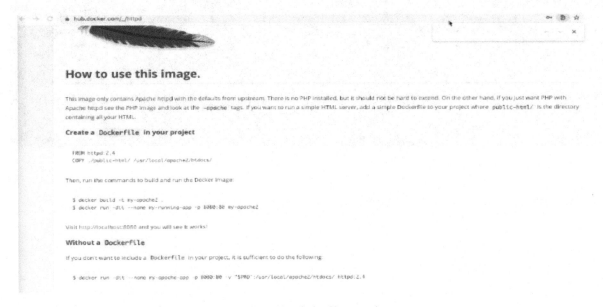

Figure 8.7 dockerfile example

Let's run the pulled httpd image. The command we will use will be:

docker run –name apache-web-server -p 8080:80 httpd

The –name switch will assign a name to the container. For example, the running instance of a Docker image is called a container or Docker container. The -p switch maps the web server's container port 80 to the local port 8080. That way, we can access a web server from outside. If we didn't do this port mapping, the running web server will not be accessible from outside.

```
sksingh:~$ docker run --name apache-web-server -p 8080:80 httpd
AH00558: httpd: Could not reliably determine the server's fully qualified domain name, using 172.17.
0.2. Set the 'ServerName' directive globally to suppress this message
AH00558: httpd: Could not reliably determine the server's fully qualified domain name, using 172.17.
0.2. Set the 'ServerName' directive globally to suppress this message
[Mon Oct 18 13:26:27.239056 2021] [mpm_event:notice] [pid 1:tid 140540183016576] AH00489: Apache/2.4
.51 (Unix) configured -- resuming normal operations
[Mon Oct 18 13:26:27.239305 2021] [core:notice] [pid 1:tid 140540183016576] AH00094: Command line: '
httpd -D FOREGROUND'
```

Figure 8.8 docker running apache-web-server docker image

Let's see if we can get the home page of the running Apache web server.

It works!

Figure 8.9 output from apache webserver running as docker container

Docker Container

As you can see from the output from the screenshot of the web browser, the Apache webserver is running inside the Docker container. So, you got the idea that a Docker container runs an instance of a Docker image.

We can stop this docker container and run it in the background. This is a good idea, and secondly, that way, we can run other Docker commands.

```
sksingh:~$ docker run --name apache-web-server -d -p 8080:80 httpd
ada5444dc1cb21040be3e84a75e76fc6922ee4c86f011430217c95476d923d0e
sksingh:~$
```

Figure 8.10 running docker container in background

Now our Apache web server's Docker container is running in the background.

List Docker Containers

Let's list all the Docker containers available in our environment: whether stopped or running. The command is: *docker ps -a*

And to list the running Docker containers, the command is:
docker container ls

```
sksingh:~$ docker container ls
CONTAINER ID    IMAGE       COMMAND             CREATED         STATUS        PORTS
NAMES
ada5444dc1cb    httpd       "httpd-foreground"  5 minutes ago   Up 5 minutes  0.0.0.0:8080->80/tcp
apache-web-server
sksingh:~$
```

Figure 8.11 docker command: docker container ls

As you can notice in the screenshot above that the running container is displayed in the output. The CONTAINER ID is 64 hex characters of the SHA-256 bit hash function. Most Docker commands truncate it to 12 characters. The next is IMAGE, which is the Docker image name. It is used in running the Docker container. The next is COMMAND. The next is when this container was created. And the next is how long this container is running. The next is PORTS. If you notice, it says it maps the local port of 8080 to the container port 80. The last one is the container name.

Connect to Running Docker Container

Now let's connect to the Docker container to find out what's inside the Docker container. The command is:
docker exec -it <container name or container id> <shell command>

In our case, it will be: *docker exec -it ada /bin/bash*

Usually, there is no need to provide all the characters of the container – the first three characters from the CONTAINER ID are sufficient.

The screenshot of the command is shown below:

```
sksingh:~$ docker exec -it ada /bin/bash
root@ada5444dc1cb:/usr/local/apache2# ls
bin  build  cgi-bin  conf  error  htdocs  icons  include  logs  modules
root@ada5444dc1cb:/usr/local/apache2# cd htdocs
root@ada5444dc1cb:/usr/local/apache2/htdocs# ls
index.html
root@ada5444dc1cb:/usr/local/apache2/htdocs# cat indea.html
cat: indea.html: No such file or directory
root@ada5444dc1cb:/usr/local/apache2/htdocs# cat index.html
<html><body><h1>It works!</h1></body></html>
root@ada5444dc1cb:/usr/local/apache2/htdocs#
```

Figure 8.12 connecting to running docker container

As you can see, after connecting to the Docker container, we ran the Linux shell ls command to list the content. Then, we cat index.html by doing cd into htdocs directory.

Stop Docker Container

First, let's come out from the Docker container by exiting out.

First list running Docker containers in the environment. The command is: *docker container ls.*

To list all the containers whether stopped or running, the Docker command is: *docker ps -a*

The command used to stop a Docker container is:
docker container stop <container id>

```
sksingh:~$ docker container stop ada
ada
sksingh:~$ docker container ls
CONTAINER ID    IMAGE      COMMAND      CREATED     STATUS      PORTS      NAMES
sksingh:~$ docker ps -a
CONTAINER ID    IMAGE      COMMAND             CREATED         STATUS                  PORTS
  NAMES
ada5444dc1cb    httpd      "httpd-foreground"  53 minutes ago  Exited (0) 19 seconds ago
  apache-web-server
sksingh:~$
```

Figure 8.13 stopping docker container

If you notice, after stopping the container, "docker container ls" is not displaying the container. However, "docker ps -a" lists the status as exited, which means the container is stopped.

We can restart this stopped container.

Restart Stopped Docker Container

The command is: *docker container start <container id>*

```
sksingh:~$ docker container start ada
ada
sksingh:~$
```

Figure 8.14 restart docker container

If you notice that the container is started, and we can access the running Docker container web server home page URL at localhost:8080.

Remove Docker Container

To remove a Docker container, the Docker container must be stopped. Then, the command to remove the docker container is:
docker container rm <container id>

The screenshot is shown below.

```
sksingh:~$ docker container rm ada
ada
sksingh:~$ docker container ls
CONTAINER ID   IMAGE       COMMAND   CREATED   STATUS    PORTS     NAMES
sksingh:~$ docker ps -a
CONTAINER ID   IMAGE       COMMAND   CREATED   STATUS    PORTS     NAMES
sksingh:~$
```

Figure 8.15 remove docker container

To remove all Docker containers from the local Docker environment:
docker rm -f $(docker ps -aq)

Remove Docker Image

The command to remove a Docker image: *docker image rm <image id>*

The output of removing the httpd image from the local Docker environment is shown below.

```
sksingh:~$ docker image rm d54
Untagged: httpd:latest
Untagged: httpd@sha256:f03a63735d3653045a3b1f5490367415e9534d8abfe0b21252454dc85ca09800
Deleted: sha256:d54056386fbb1ea69f9332f35ab083dd7062cc9cb78ed28ce6b8f85e9dfb56b3
Deleted: sha256:cb81287bdd44f4b08efb2c7f068254354e194b324d257ab71dbdeb26184b7acd
Deleted: sha256:f74cf2cff8b0d46087a99a5fa25b7be47a8f8b652aa648f7f881c352a8538f38
Deleted: sha256:5e8d63300ef030c0584071a54aef969a1ef064d7820b5816740d8c3d164acec0
Deleted: sha256:91e725bc196deb57684d97ee89c115b1d9b2470b7c0bdac585f473eb7d306a88
Deleted: sha256:e81bff2725dbc0bf2003db10272fef362e882eb96353055778a66cda430cf81b
sksingh:~$ docker image ls
REPOSITORY   TAG         IMAGE ID   CREATED   SIZE
sksingh:~$
```

Figure 8.16 remove docker image

How to Build Docker Image

In the previous use case, we pulled the httpd Docker image and ran the Apache web server using that image as a Docker container. When you are working on an application or have a DevOps role, many times you will have to create custom Docker images. The reason is each application has its dependencies, components it needs, and runtime configurations.

For example, say if you have a typical 3-tier web application with a data, server, and UI layer. Then depending on how you have designed your application, you may need MySQL image, MongoDB image, Kafka Image, Node.JS image, and application source codes. Of course, I'm just assuming images here. Your web application may have been built using some other tools, libraries, and frameworks. I hope you got the idea that to build the Docker image of your application. You will have to create a Docker image.

Creating Docker Images

Now, we will learn how to create Docker images. First, we will create a Docker image using an httpd image from Docker Hub. To create a Docker image. First, we need to create a Dockerfile. Dockerfile contains all the other images, dependencies, and commands. I'm using office httpd documentation to build the httpd Docker image.

Create a Dockerfile in your project

```
FROM httpd:2.4
COPY ./public-html/ /usr/local/apache2/htdocs/
```

I have created a public-html directory and added index.html.

```
sksingh:~/myDockerDemo$ cd public-html/
sksingh:~/myDockerDemo/public-html$ cat index.html
<html>
 This is local index.html
<html>
sksingh:~/myDockerDemo/public-html$
```

Let me add Dockerfile in the directory where I have public-html dir.

```
sksingh:~$ cd myDockerDemo/
sksingh:~/myDockerDemo$ vi Dockerfile
sksingh:~/myDockerDemo$ cat Dockerfile
FROM httpd:2.4
COPY ./public-html/ /usr/local/apache2/htdocs/
sksingh:~/myDockerDemo$
```

Figure 8.17 dockerfile creation

Now let's build this image.

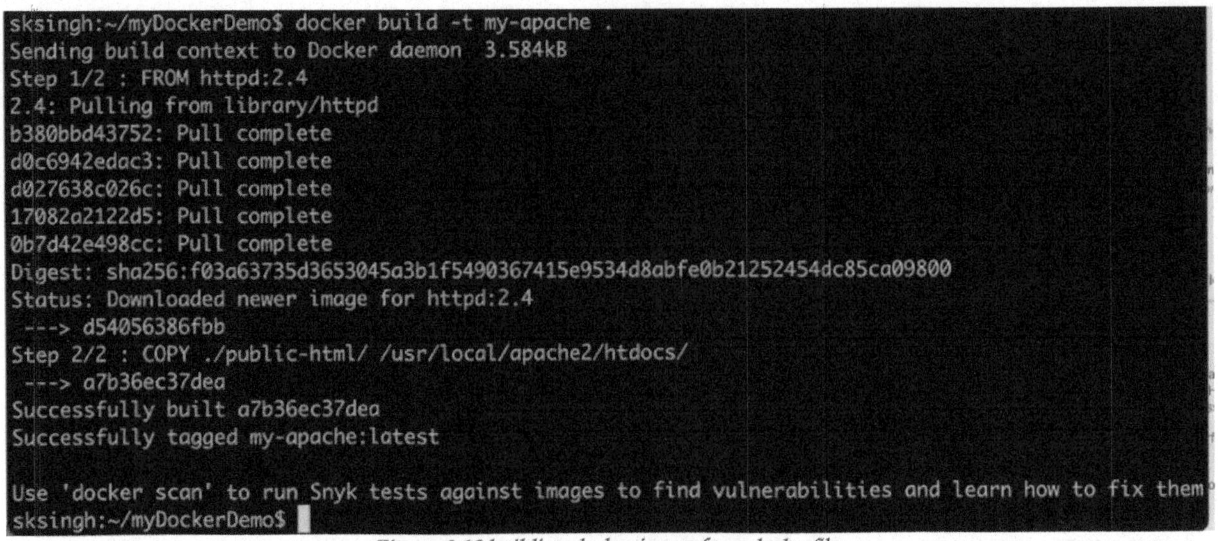

Figure 8.18 building docker image from dockerfile

You may have to run this command if the docker build is giving error: "Failed to resolve with frontend ..."

export DOCKER_BUILDKIT=0
export COMPOSE_DOCKER_CLI_BUILD=0

The Docker image has been created from the Dockerfile. Now let's see if we can find this image in our Docker environment.

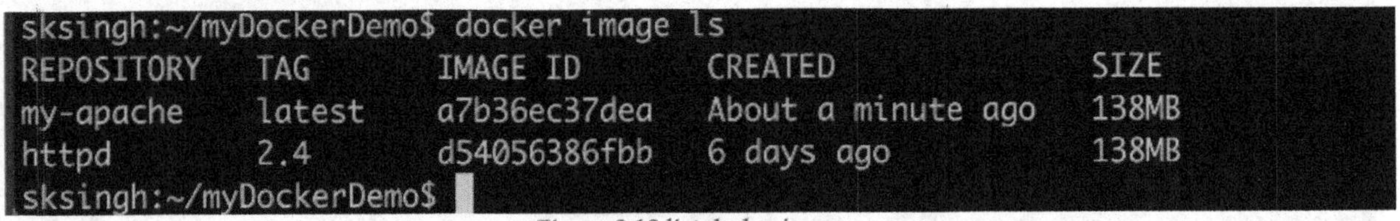

Figure 8.19 list docker images

Yes, we can see two images; one is official, and the other one is created by running the Dockerfile. Now let's run this Docker image and see if you can get an output of HTTP server.

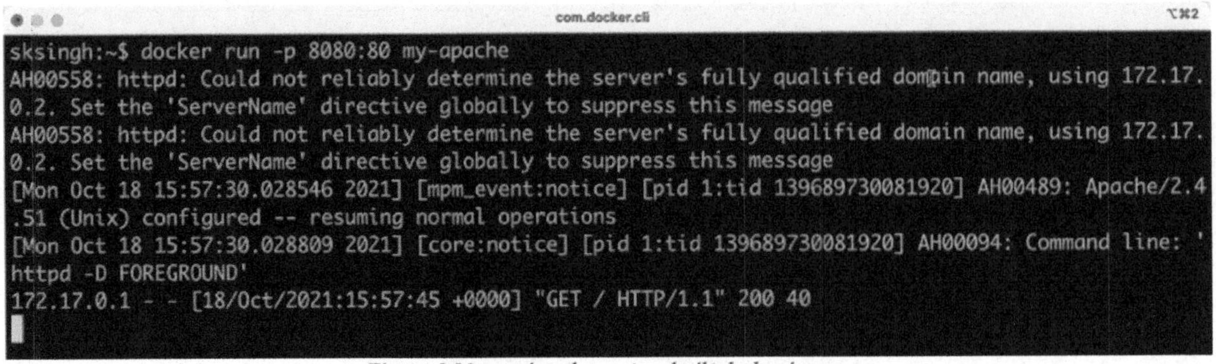

Figure 8.20 running the custom built docker image

Cloud Computing and AWS Introduction

This is local index.html

Figure 8.21 output of running the webserver docker image

As you can notice, based on the screenshot we got the output of running our first custom Docker image using Dockerfile.

Push Docker Image to Docker Hub

Sign Up to Docker Hub

Figure 8.22 docker hub sign up

To push Docker images to Docker Hub, first, you need to sign up on hubs.docker.com Once you have signed up, click on the "Continue with Free" button. It will ask you to verify email address,

Create Repository

Next, click on the repository and will create a repository to store the Docker "my-apache" image, which is the custom Docker image name that I used when building that Docker image.

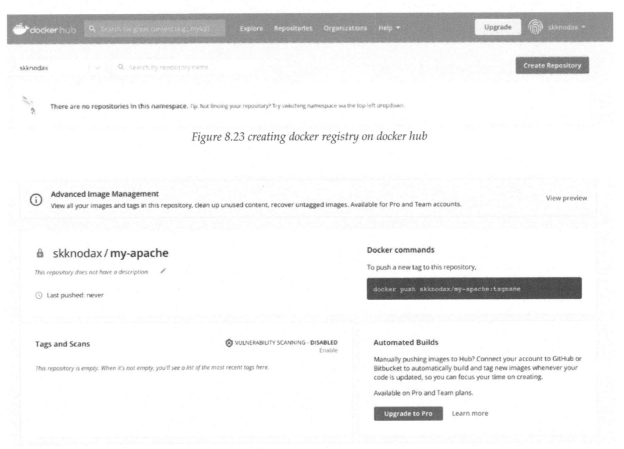

Figure 8.23 creating docker registry on docker hub

Figure 8.24 docker registry created on docker hub

The repository skknodax/my-apache has been created, as you can see in the screenshot.

Push Docker Image to the Docker Hub

Make sure the Docker image name also includes your user id. For example, I rebuilt the image to provide the tag name, which is skknodax/my-apache:latest

docker build -t skknodax/my-apache:latest .

```
sksingh:~/myDockerDemo$ docker build -t skknodax/my-apache:latest .
Sending build context to Docker daemon  3.584kB
Step 1/2 : FROM httpd:2.4
 ---> d54056386fbb
Step 2/2 : COPY ./public-html/ /usr/local/apache2/htdocs/
 ---> Using cache
 ---> a7b36ec37dea
Successfully built a7b36ec37dea
Successfully tagged skknodax/my-apache:latest
```

Figure 8.25 build docker image

Next, you need to log in to Docker using docker login.

```
sksingh:~/myDockerDemo$ docker login
Login with your Docker ID to push and pull images from Docker Hub. If you don't have a Docker ID, he
ad over to https://hub.docker.com to create one.
Username: skknodax
Password:
Login Succeeded
```

Figure 8.26 login to docker hub

Then run the docker push command:
docker push skknodax/my-apache:latest

You can see in the screenshot.

```
sksingh:~/myDockerDemo$ docker push skknodax/my-apache:latest
The push refers to repository [docker.io/skknodax/my-apache]
a7f6a2485833: Pushed
05e8e8829257: Mounted from library/httpd
cff5df9a17ba: Mounted from library/httpd
3e53444292eb: Mounted from library/httpd
dc9cff0c1004: Mounted from library/httpd
e81bff2725db: Mounted from library/httpd
latest: digest: sha256:193bea9c5d6417ce9f9f70ac617b0d5afc97bc73e9b4cfbde062c998057ad659 size: 1573
sksingh:~/myDockerDemo$
```

Figure 8.27 push docker image to docker hub

This is the screenshot where the image is pushed to the Docker Hub.

Figure 8.28 docker image pushed on the docker hub

Pull the Docker image from the Private Repository

Remove all the Docker images, first. This is just to have a clean local environment.

```
sksingh:~$ docker system prune -a
WARNING! This will remove:
    - all stopped containers
    - all networks not used by at least one container
    - all images without at least one container associated to them
    - all build cache

Are you sure you want to continue? [y/N] y
Deleted Containers:
3e071893147c333a4b05e49be80f545f8442788f727ae325d7f8bc13fd52e452
9b9443b858489eaee239c1f4d0b1616799753e5d4dc3439c3b3d447a8b01ef34

Deleted Images:
untagged: my-apache:latest
untagged: skknodax/my-apache:latest
untagged: skknodax/my-apache@sha256:193bea9c5d6417ce9f9f70ac617b0d5afc97bc73e9b4cfbde062c998057ad659
untagged: sksingh/my-apache:latest
deleted: sha256:a7b36ec37dea3d5c5257f7c42cf2145b7cd752e233f4ae68a435a254f22e5663
deleted: sha256:e29ccbb1194f591372b187023abe281e26f7cdf8ba5113a736689880231c410a
untagged: httpd:2.4
untagged: httpd@sha256:f03a63735d3653045a3b1f5490367415e9534d8abfe0b21252454dc85ca09800
deleted: sha256:d54056386fbb1ea69f9332f35ab083dd7062cc9cb78ed28ce6b8f85e9dfb56b3
deleted: sha256:cb81287bdd44f4b08efb2c7f068254354e194b324d257ab71dbdeb26184b7acd
deleted: sha256:f74cf2cff8b0d46087a99a5fa25b7be47a8f8b652aa648f7f881c352a8538f38
deleted: sha256:5e8d63300ef030c0584071a54aef969a1ef064d7820b5816740d8c3d164acec0
deleted: sha256:91e725bc196deb57684d97ee89c115b1d9b2470b7c0bdac585f473eb7d306a88
deleted: sha256:e81bff2725dbc0bf2003db10272fef362e882eb96353055778a66cda430cf81b

Total reclaimed space: 138MB
sksingh:~$
```

Figure 8.29 removing all the images from the docker local environment

There are no Docker images on my local docker environment:

```
Total reclaimed space: 138MB
sksingh:~$ docker image ls
REPOSITORY     TAG        IMAGE ID   CREATED   SIZE
sksingh:~$
```

Figure 8.30 docker image listing

Now, pull the Docker image which is pushed on the private repository.

```
sksingh:~$ docker image ls
REPOSITORY     TAG        IMAGE ID      CREATED     SIZE
sksingh:~$ docker pull skknodax/my-apache
Using default tag: latest
latest: Pulling from skknodax/my-apache
b380bbd43752: Pull complete
d0c6942edac3: Pull complete
d027638c026c: Pull complete
17082a2122d5: Pull complete
0b7d42e498cc: Pull complete
52b551bd4dd9: Pull complete
Digest: sha256:193bea9c5d6417ce9f9f70ac617b0d5afc97bc73e9b4cfbde062c998057ad659
Status: Downloaded newer image for skknodax/my-apache:latest
docker.io/skknodax/my-apache:latest
sksingh:~$ docker image ls
REPOSITORY           TAG        IMAGE ID      CREATED           SIZE
skknodax/my-apache   latest     a7b36ec37dea  About an hour ago  138MB
sksingh:~$
```

Figure 8.31 pull docker image from the docker hub

As you can notice in the screenshot that the image has been pulled. Now, I can run this private image to set up a web server in a Docker container as discussed earlier.

We did a small exercise of setting up a webserver using a Docker container. During this exercise, we learned many Docker concepts and many Docker commands. Now let's go through some common Docker terms, which you will encounter when using Docker.

Docker Terms

Dockerfile

It is a text document containing all the commands to build a Docker image, including operating system libraries, application source code, and dependencies. These commands are like Linux command line commands, as you can notice in a Dockerfile given below in a screenshot. The Dockerfile in the screenshot gets the latest Ubuntu image, updates the image, installs OpenJDK version 8. Then copies the jar file into /usr/local/bin directory. And finally sets an entry point to run the jar file.

Figure 8.32 dockerfile script

Docker Image

The Dockerfile contains the source code of a Docker image, as you can see in the image above. Once you have Dockerfile, you build the docker image from the Dockerfile by running the Docker command docker build. Thus, you could think of the docker image as a compiled version of Dockerfile. Docker images you can push to Docker Hub, which is a Docker registry, for redistribution.

Docker Container

Docker containers are runtime instances of Docker images. When you apply the command "docker run <Docker Image Name>," it creates a Docker container of that image which is the run time instance of the Docker image. You can stop the Docker container, restart it or remove it.

Docker Hub

Docker Hub is a registry provided by Docker to maintain and distribute Docker images. After building a Docker image, you can push it to the Docker Hub if you would like to share it with the public.

Docker Overview

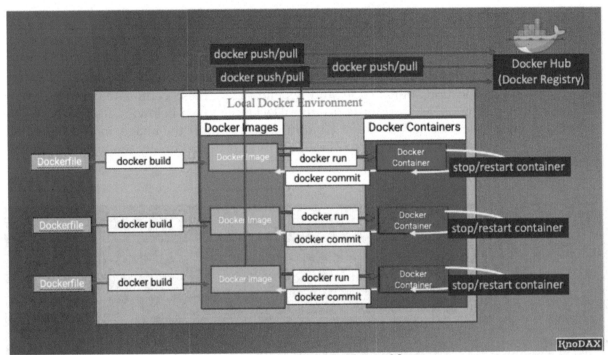

Figure 8.33 docker typical DevOps workflow

Let's get a high-level understanding of the Docker system based on this diagram. In this diagram, you notice there is a Dockerfile. Depending on your applications, you may have many Dockerfiles to build custom Docker images.

Then you run docker build command to build Docker images from the Dockerfile. Once the images are built you can run Docker containers from the Docker images. If you would like to push the images, can push images to Docker Hub. If you can also pull images from Docker Hub. You can stop and restart the stopped Docker container. You can also apply a docker commit to save the image if the Docker container is modified.

Most Useful Docker Commands

Docker Build

```
$ docker build [OPTIONS] PATH | URL | -
```

The docker build command builds a Docker image from Dockerfile.

Docker Push

```
$ docker push [OPTIONS] NAME[:TAG]
```

The docker push command pushes the Docker image to the Docker registry. The default Docker registry is Docker Hub.

Docker Pull

```
$ docker pull [OPTIONS] NAME[:TAG|@DIGEST]
```

The docker pull command pulls the Docker image from the Docker registry. The default Docker registry is Docker Hub.

Docker Run

```
$ docker run [OPTIONS] IMAGE [COMMAND] [ARG...]
```

The docker run command runs the Docker image.

Docker Stop / Start

```
$ docker stop [OPTIONS] CONTAINER [CONTAINER...]
```

The docker stop command stops the running Docker container.

```
$ docker start [OPTIONS] CONTAINER [CONTAINER...]
```

The docker start command start the stopped Docker container.

Docker Exec

```
$ docker exec [OPTIONS] CONTAINER COMMAND [ARG...]
```

The docker exec is used to connect to Docker container.

Docker List Images

```
$ docker images [OPTIONS] [REPOSITORY[:TAG]]
```

The docker image ls command is used to list Docker images.

Docker List Containers
The docker container ls command is used to list Docker containers.

Docker Remove Image

docker image rm <image id>

To remove all Docker images: docker system prune -a

Docker Remove Container

docker container rm <container id>

To remove all containers: docker rm -f $(docker ps -aq)

Docker Commit
The docker commit command is used to save the current running state of the Docker container as an image. Essentially, the command creates a new image from a container's changes.

```
$ docker commit [OPTIONS] CONTAINER [REPOSITORY[:TAG]]
```

Related YouTube Video
Introduction to Docker: https://youtu.be/baieX04jB8s

Chapter Review Questions

Exercise

1. Please follow the video: Introduction to Docker: https://youtu.be/baieX04jB8s to set up a web server on Docker.

For the questions given below, please mark them if they are true or false.

2. Docker is an open platform Virtualization technology. True / False

3. The docker pull command pulls a Docker image from the local repository. True / False

4. The docker run command runs a docker image and running the docker container can be listed by running the command docker container ls. True / False

5. The "docker image ls" lists docker images available on the local docker environment. True / False

6. Docker Hub is a public Docker repository. True / False

Part II: AWS Introduction

aws

AWS is a Cloud Service Provider

Chapter 9. What is AWS?

Congratulations on completing the Cloud Computing section, and Welcome to the AWS section of the book. Since you have got a good understanding of cloud computing from the first section, you will find this section easier to comprehend. First, we will start with an introduction to AWS, which will set up the momentum for the rest of the section.

Cloud Services Provider

Figure 9.0.1 what is AWS

What is AWS? AWS is a public cloud service provider, and its architectural underpinning is based on cloud computing.

AWS provides almost all kinds of cloud services such as infrastructure, platform, software, analytics, machine learning, and many other types of services over the Internet. These cloud services are highly reliable, scalable, and low-cost. AWS is an evolving cloud computing platform, and new services of different types are continuously getting added. It is a cloud computing platform to procure, deploy, and manage IT Infrastructure. Additionally, AWS is a secure modern platform to build, deploy, and run almost all kinds of software applications. Most importantly, it does it with time and cost-efficiency.

AWS Use Cases

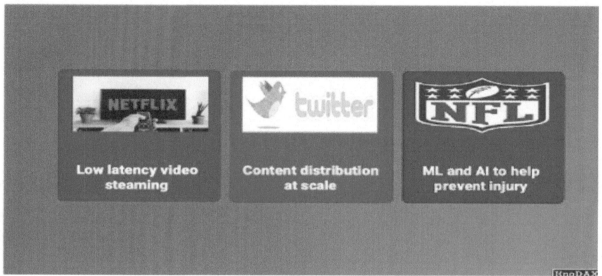

Figure 9.2 AWS use cases

To understand further what AWS is, let's see some interesting use cases of AWS. Did you know how Netflix is streaming videos worldwide with low latency? Netflix uses AWS to achieve low latency performance. Have you ever wondered how Twitter can scale its distribution of content worldwide? Twitter uses the AWS platform to scale its distribution worldwide. Did you happen to know how NFL is leveraging AI and machine learning to predict and prevent injury in games? NFL is leveraging AWS machine learning and AI services to expect and to avoid damage in matches.

AWS Customers

Figure 9.3 AWS customers

Now we have gone through a few use cases of AWS. Continuing further on what AWS is, let's try to understand AWS in terms of its customers. AWS has over a million customers in around 190 countries as of this writing. it has customers from organizations of all types, such as large, medium, and startups in various industries. Regarding companies that are using AWS, some well-known organizations that have big spending on AWS are Facebook, BBC News, ESPN, LinkedIn, GE, and Apple.

How AWS Compares with Other Cloud Providers

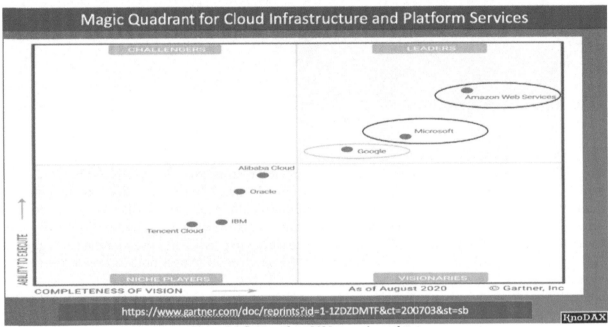

Figure 9.4 Gartner chart 2020 -- magic quadrant

Let's see how AWS compares with the other cloud providers. The Gartner chart of 2020 given below gives a clear picture of different cloud providers in terms of "completeness of vision" and "ability to execute." In this chart, the X-axis represents "Completes of Vision," and "Ability to Execute" is mentioned on the Y-axis. You can notice Amazon Web Services is the leader on both axes. Microsoft is on 2nd, and Google is on 3rd. The other cloud providers such as Oracle and IBM are way behind.

Different Types of Services AWS Offers

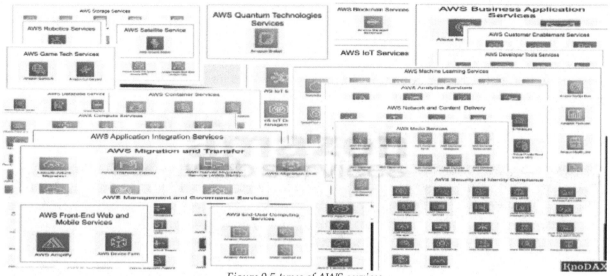

Figure 9.5 types of AWS services

Different Types of AWS Services

AWS provides services in 25 categories:
- Analytics
- Application Integration
- AR & VR
- Blockchain
- Business Applications
- Compute
- Containers
- Cost Management
- Customer Enablement
- Database
- Developer Tools
- End-User Computing
- Front End and Mobile
- Game Tech
- Internet of Things
- Machine Learning
- Management & Governance
- Media Services
- Migration & Transfer
- Networking & Content Delivery
- Quantum Technologies
- Robotics

- Satellite
- Security Identity & Compliance
- Storage

AWS Advantages

Let's try to understand AWS advantages, which would help us rationalize why AWS has become such a popular and valuable platform in the computing world.

Don't have to Buy Any Special Hardware

Figure 9.6 AWS advantages -- available over the Internet

One of the advantages is that AWS services or any cloud services for that matter are available over the Internet, which is a considerable advantage over on-premises. We don't have to buy or maintain any special hardware to use AWS.

Cost Savings

Figure 9.7 AWS advantages -- cost savings

Another advantage is cost savings. AWS pricing model is based on pay-for-what-you-use. This pricing model helps cut down a lot in cost in many use cases, mainly when we don't fully utilize the bought resources. In other words, in the scenarios where resources are idle most of the time, AWS is advantageous with respect to cost savings.

Let's see some use case examples to get a better idea about cost savings advantage.

Figure 9.8 cost savings: Valentine's Day use case

Say our business sells gift items only related to Valentine's Day, then running our online store on high-end webservers with auto-scaling and load balancer would find it challenging to do a profitable business throughout a year.

On the other hand, if we can leverage AWS, we will only pay for the services we use, thus having a potentially profitable business. Leveraging a cloud computing platform such as AWS with a pay-for-what-you-use pricing model saves enormous costs, as you only pay for what you use.

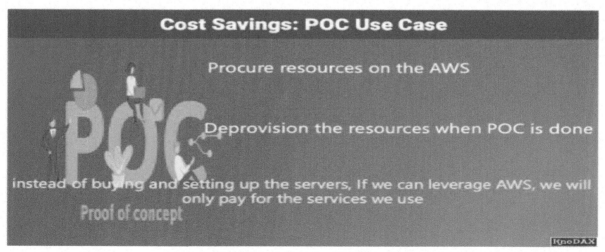

Figure 9.9 cost savings: POC use case

This pay-for-what-you-use pricing model is very cost-effective and becoming a new paradigm in the computing world.

In another example, suppose we need some special servers to work on some urgent proof of concepts, aka POC type of work, to add some features in our product, which our competitor doesn't have. And say, after the POC is complete, we don't need the computing resources.

In this business use case, instead of buying and setting up the servers, if we can leverage AWS, we will only pay for the services we use, which is the price for running the virtual servers on AWS. As you can see, leveraging AWS in this use case would lead us to cost savings.

Time Savings

Figure 9.10 AWS advantages: time savings

Additionally, it saves time as well. Since setting up networking, security, permissions, etc., are relatively much easier and more robust on AWS.

Ease of Use

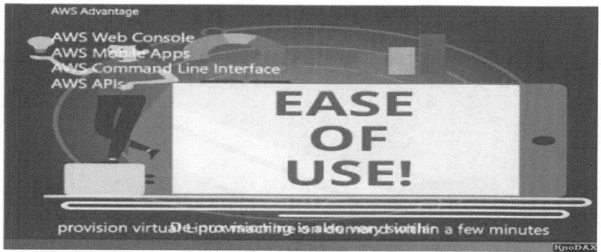

Figure 9.11 AWS advantages: ease of use

Not only cost savings, but AWS is also easy to use, as well. With AWS, we can provision and manage all sorts of computing resources with various choices. We can use AWS Web Console, AWS Mobile Apps, AWS Command Line Interface, and AWS APIs. For example, we can provision virtual Linux machines on demand within a few minutes. De-provisioning is also very similar -- we can deprovision or unwind provisioned resources quickly, like how we provisioned the computing resources.

AWS Cloud History

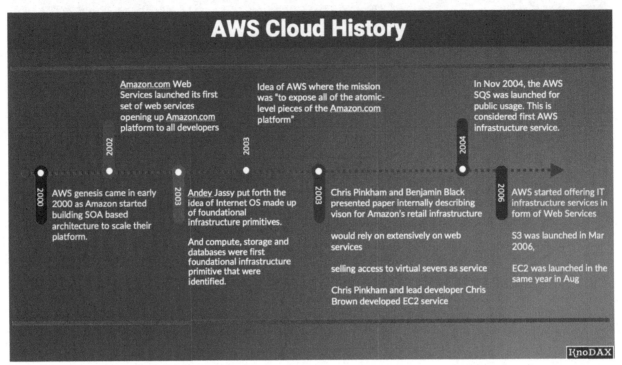

AWS genesis came in early 2000 as Amazon started building SOA-based architecture to scale their platform. Around that time, Amazon was launching its e-commerce platform for third-party retailers to make a web store for their retail stores. This effort of launching an e-commerce platform for third-party retailers led to the demand for a more scalable system.

Then in 2002, Amazon.com Web Services launched its first set of web services, opening the Amazon.com platform to all developers. The most exciting story is that Amazon was caught by surprise by its developers' unexpected interest in web service API.

Then in 2003, Andy Jassy, who is CEO now, put forth the idea of Internet OS made up of foundational infrastructure primitives. The first foundational infrastructure primitives -- compute, storage, and databases -- were identified. Based on this idea, Jeff Barr, Jassy, Bezos himself, and others formulated the concept of EC2 for computing, S3 for storage, and RDS for the database. These three are very famous AWS services now.

This [2003] was an essential year for AWS. In fact, according to Amazon Web Services Wiki, Jassy recalls brainstorming sessions for about a week with ten of the best technology minds and ten of the best product management minds on about ten different internet applications, the most primitive blocks required to build them. That discussion and other related events paved the idea of AWS, where the mission was to expose all the atomic-level pieces of the Amazon.com platform.

In 2003, Chris Pinkham and Benjamin Black presented a paper internally describing the vision for Amazon's retail infrastructure that was overhauling Amazon retail infrastructure to be completely automated and would rely extensively on web services. The paper also mentioned the possibility of selling access to virtual servers as a service and proposed that the company

Cloud Computing and AWS Introduction

generate revenue from the new infrastructure investment. And after that, Chris Pinkham and lead developer Chris Brown developed the EC2 Service.

In Nov 2004, the AWS SQS was launched for public usage. This is considered the first AWS infrastructure service.

After that, in 2006, AWS started offering IT infrastructure services in Web Services. S3 was launched in Mar 2006, and EC2 was launched in the same year in Aug. Over the years, many more services have been added to the AWS platform. AWS is an evolving platform – more and more features and services are continuously added to its platform.

As of this writing, AWS has over 200 products and services in almost all possible categories where AWS can offer its services.

Summary

To summarize, AWS helps in cost savings, time savings. it is easy to use as well. Moreover, we don't need to buy any special hardware to use AWS. It has over a million active customers, and readily available all kinds of cloud services. AWS has a pay-for-what-you-use pricing model.

It is a cloud computing platform to build, deploy, and run almost all kinds of software applications. It is also a cloud computing platform to procure, deploy, and manage IT infrastructure with time and cost-efficiency. Today AWS provides highly reliable, scalable low-cost cloud services from its cloud computing platform.

Related YouTube Videos

What is AWS: https://youtu.be/R6sZxyxpM5w
Types of Services: https://youtu.be/X3Dhs3CnaGc
AWS Advantages: https://youtu.be/3eF7mAeJpz0

Chapter Review Questions

For the questions given below, please mark them if they are true or false.

1. AWS provides almost all kinds of cloud services such as infrastructure, platform, software, analytics, machine learning, and many other types of services over the Internet. True / False

Please select the correct answer from the given choices for the questions below.

2.   In which of the following categories does AWS provide services?

    a. Blockchain
    b. Internet of Things (IoT)
    c. Machine Learning
    d. all of them

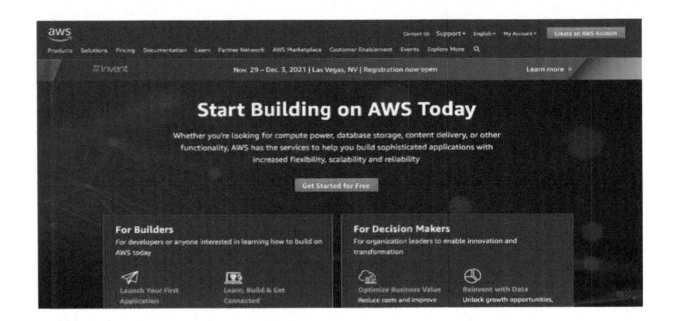

Chapter 10. AWS Account

The theory is good to set up the conceptual understanding of AWS. However, the best way to learn AWS services is to know them by doing. If you plan to learn AWS in more detail and prepare for AWS certifications, learning AWS services hands-on will be very useful. Nonetheless, I have heard that hands-on learning helps improve retention. In the chapter, we will learn many aspects of AWS account by doing hands-on, such as signing up for an AWS account, securing your AWS account, AWS Free Tier, and setting up AWS budget alarm.

Sign Up for AWS Account

Now you have got an understanding about what AWS is. Let's sign up for an AWS account so that you can learn AWS services. If you already have an AWS account, then you can skip this part of the chapter.

Step 1: Basic Information

First, head to https://aws.amazon.com, and click on the "Create an AWS Account." button. It will take you to the "Sign-Up for AWS" page.

Figure 10.0.1 AWS account sign-up

On this page, enter your email address. Please make sure you provide the correct email address. The email address will become your AWS user id. Enter password, re-enter the password. Provide AWS Account name. It will be used on your AWS billing -- You can change this name in your account settings after you sign up. Click on the Continue button.

Step 2: Address

Now on this page, it asks if this account is a Professional or a Personal account. Please select Personal, which is mostly a common choice.

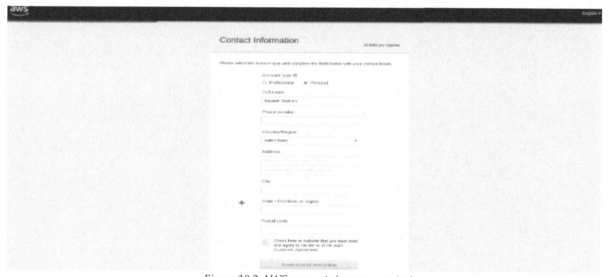

Figure 10.2 AWS account sign up -- contact

On this page, please enter details: full name, phone number, and address. Then, check the customer agreement checkbox -- you can read the details before checking the checkbox. Then, click on the Continue button.

Step 3: Billing

On this page, enter billing information. And then, click on the "Verify and Add" button.

Figure 10.3 AWS account sign up -- payment

Step 4: Identity Verification

It will take you to the page asking for a mobile number or voice call for verification. Please check the text message option, which is a common choice. You will need to provide a phone number.

Figure 10.4 AWS account sign up – identity verification

Step 5: Identity Verification Code

On this page, enter the code which you got.

Figure 10.5 AWS account sign up – identity verification code

Step 6: Identity Verification Complete

If the code is verified, you will get the confirmation screen for the verification completion. Then, click on the "Continue" button, which will take you to the "Select a Plan Selection" page.

Step 7: Support Plan Selection

The "Select a Support Plan" page asks which type of support plans you would like to have.

Primarily for learning or trying out services for preparing certification exams, the Basic Plan option is sufficient– as it is free.

Figure 10.6 AWS account sign up -- support plan selection

Essentially in the Basic Plan, you will leverage AWS documentation to get help if you get stuck. In my personal experience, Basic Plan is fine for learning or preparing for certification exams. You will need the Developer Plan option if you need to contact someone in AWS to help solve your AWS issue. Essentially, you will create a support ticket in this option if you have any support-related questions, and the AWS support team will handle your support ticket. The Business Plan is typically used by businesses using AWS to get help on their AWS issue.

Step 8: Account is Setup

Once you select a support plan, you will get an email from AWS about your account setup.

Figure 10.7 AWS account sign-up complete

You can log in to start using AWS.

Figure 10.8 AWS account sign up -- welcome screen

Budget Alarm Set Up

Before using AWS, one of the critical tasks is setting up a budget alarm to help keep your AWS bills within the check.

AWS has a Free Tier -- then why do I need to set up a budget alarm?

Typically for preparing AWS certification exam, it's good practice to use the services given in the AWS Free Tier. AWS Free Tier is a feature provided by AWS to try out and learn AWS services free of cost for some time, typically for one year. However, the free tier will not be sufficient to learn and try out the services if you are seriously preparing for the AWS Solutions Architect exam. For example, my AWS bill for preparing certification was around $15.

So, by setting up the budget alarm, you make sure to get some sort of notification such as email or text, depending on what you have configured if you're exceeding the budget threshold. The budget alarm will help in keeping your AWS bills within your budget.

That being said, let's go ahead to set up the budget alarm.

Step 1: Billing Dashboard

In the search bar, type billing to easily find the "Billing & Cost Management Dashboard" if you have previously visited this service, it will be shown on your home page once you logged in.

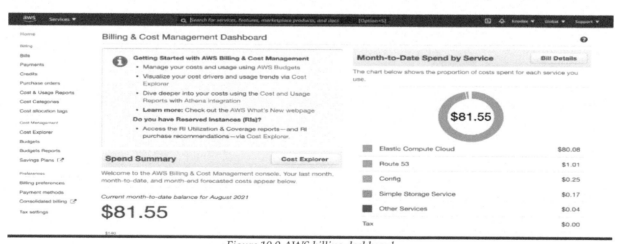

Figure 10.9 AWS billing dashboard

Step 2: Create Budget

Once you are on the "Billing & Cost Management Dashboard" page, here click on the Budget link on the left sidebar. You will get the Overview page.

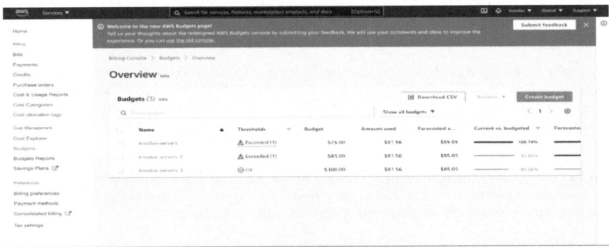

Figure 10.10 billing & cost management -- overview

On the Overview page, click on the Create Budget button which is at the top right side.

Figure 10.11 AWS billing & dashboard --choose budget type

It will take you to the "Choose budget type" page. Select a budget type, which is cost budget.

Step 3: Set your budget

Figure 10.12 AWS billing & dashboard -- set your budget

Click next, and for the period, select monthly, and select recurring for the budget effective date. Set the starting month, and then enter the budget amount, for example, $1.00. Enter budget name, for example, "AWS Certification Preparation Budget," and then click Next.

On the next screen, enter threshold -- 80% is typical. Next, enter the email where you would like to get the notification. Please make sure you provide the correct email address.

Figure 10.13 AWS billing & cost management -- budget amount

AWS Root Account Best Practices

It is an important topic! In this, I'll cover best practices for AWS root account, which are very important for the security and safety of your AWS Root Account.

Let's go through the best practices to keep in mind concerning the AWS root account.

- DO NOT SHARE YOUR ROOT ACCOUNT AND PASSWORD WITH ANYONE
- Secure your root account by MULTI-FACTOR AUTHENTICATION
- DO NOT USE ROOT ACCOUNT USER ID to log in as this is a highly privileged account. Additionally, using a root account for regular use can increase the security risk of the account.
- CREATE ANOTHER ACCOUNT AND USE THIS ACCOUNT for everyday use.

The key takeaway is to have an AWS root account or any AWS account for that matter EXTREMELY SECURE AND DO NOT LEAK OR EXPOSE YOUR AWS ACCOUNT PASSWORD AND ACCESS KEYS!

How to Add Multi-Factor Authentication (MFA)

What is MFA?

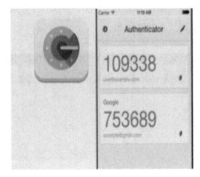

Multi-factor authentication, or in short, MFA, is an electronic authentication method in which a user is granted access to a website or application only after successfully presenting two or more pieces of evidence to an authentication mechanism: knowledge, possession, and inherence.
(Source: https://en.wikipedia.org/wiki/Multi-factor_authentication)

Figure 10.14 what is MFA

MFA for Security and Safety of Your AWS Account

Adding multi-factor authentication is a critical task with respect to the security and safety of your AWS account. Usually, in organizations, it is done by the system administrator. However, if you have a personal AWS account, you should make sure you have added MFA before using your AWS account. Therefore, it is highly recommended to add MFA to your AWS account before you start using the AWS account.

Different Ways MFA Can be Added to Your AWS Account

In AWS, MFA can be added using three different mechanisms:
- Virtual MFA Device

- U2F (Universal 2 Factor) Security Key

- Hardware MFA Device

Virtual MFA Device

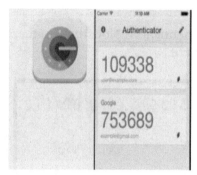

MFA device is easy to set up. For example, you can install Authenticator App such as Google Authenticator, 1Password, Microsoft Authenticator on your mobile device. And use the code generated on the app to log in along with the password.

Figure 10.15 virtual MFA device

How secure is it?

Now the question is how secure it is. It is secure, but it also has potential for security risk – but not as weak as using SMS for MFA. As we know, SMS is another two-factor authentication mechanism. But in SMS, the text is transmitted unencrypted. As you can see, SMS is weaker compared to the authenticator app for MFA.

There is a blog post:

https://www.zdnet.com/article/using-google-authenticator-heres-why-you-should-get-rid-of-it/

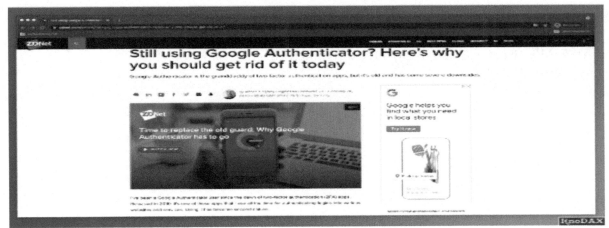

Figure 10.16 google authenticator related blog post

You can read about this blog post to know more about Google Authenticator. Nonetheless, there is this paragraph in this blog post, which I would like to mention here.

Another drawback of Google Authenticator that a reader pointed out is no passcode or biometric lock on the app. And this ease of access to the app seems to allow malware to steal 2FA codes directly from Google Authenticator, giving you yet another good reason to dump the app.

Figure 10.17 google authenticator blog post -- highlighted comment

From the post, you can see that Google Authenticator doesn't seem to be very safe. So, depending on how critical your AWS account is, Google Authenticator may not be the right choice for you -- though it is quick and easy to set up.

U2F (Universal 2 Factor) Security Key

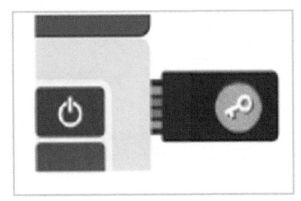

Figure 10.18 U2F (Universal 2 Factor)

The other choice is U2F, which is a shorter form of Universal 2 Factor. Authenticator apps are safer than 2-factor authentication via SMS, as SMS messages are transmitted as unencrypted. However, authenticator apps are not as secure as using a U2F device.

U2F is the type of MFA device, which you can plug into a USB port. Once you enable it using the instructions that follow, you just tap it on the device when prompted to log in securely. Tapping helps make sure some human is logging – not a robot.

It is based on RSA, which, as you might know, RSA is public and private key cryptography. But the concept is relatively modern. U2F device key and hardware of the computer are used to generate keys.

If someone gets your U2F device, they can't use it to log in to your site as nothing is stored on the U2F device. However, they can use that device for themselves to log in to websites – but not on your websites.

The only drawback is that if you lost your device, you need to have a backup system to log into.

Hardware MFA Device

And the third option is to use hardware MFA devices. The concept is like the SecureID if you have used it. First, you register the device, and then, when prompted, enter the token generated on the device.

Figure 10.19 hardware MFA device

How to Add MFA Using Google Authenticator

Step 1. Log in to AWS

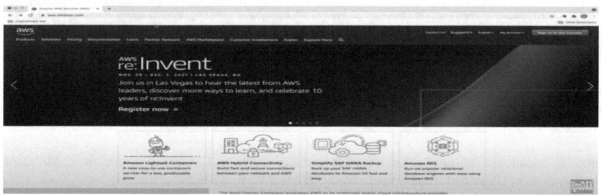

Figure 10.20 log in to AWS

Step 2. Go to My Security Credential, which is under your account name.

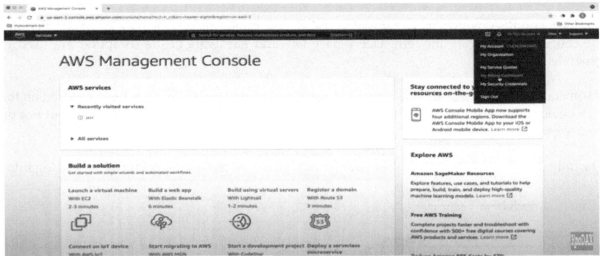

Figure 10.21 my security credential

Step 3. Click on Multi-factor Authentication, and then click on the Activate MFA.

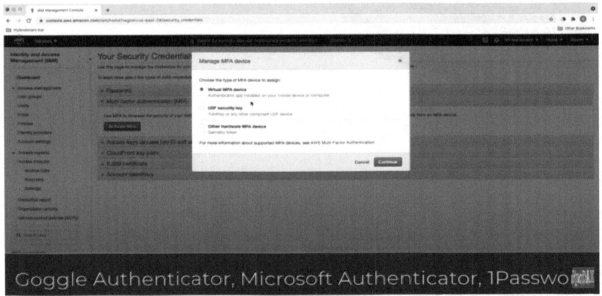

Figure 10.22 manage MFA device

Here there are three choices. The first one is the Virtual MFA device. The other choices are "U2F security key" and "other hardware MFA device." Let's use a virtual MFA device, which is commonly used. Though it is not as secure as the other two choices, it's quick and easy to set up.

Step 4. Install any authenticator on your mobiles such as Google Authenticator, Microsoft Authenticator, 1Pasword. And you are ready to use a Virtual MFA device.

Step 5. Once you have installed the authenticator app, click on the Continue button. I'm using Google Authenticator to explain this setup.

Step 6. On the next screen, scan the QR code on your mobile and enter the two consecutive codes displayed on your mobile for verification. Then click on the Assign MFA button.

Figure 10.23 scan QR code

Step 7. Then, you will get the message that you have successfully assigned the MFA to your account.

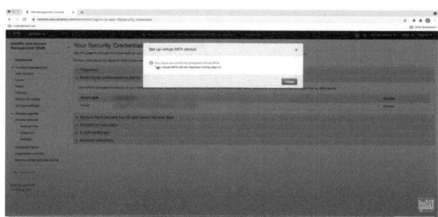

Figure 10.24 MFA assignment confirmation

AWS Free Tier

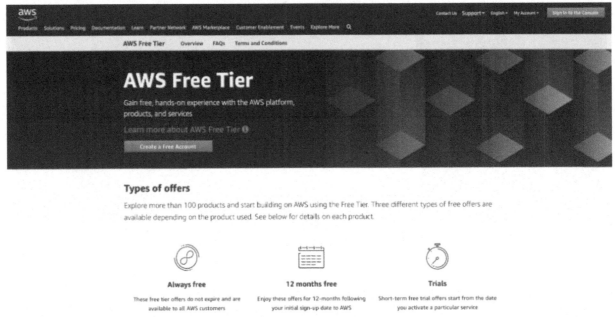

Figure 10.25 AWS Free Tier home page

AWS Free Tier (https://aws.amazon.com/free) is a feature provided by AWS to try out and learn AWS services free of charge within certain usage limits, for some time, typically for one year. The AWS Free Tier is automatically activated on each new AWS account.

There are three types of offers available in AWS Free Tier:

Always Free

Always Free offers do not expire at the end of your 12-month AWS Free Tier term and are available to all AWS customers.

12 Months Free

You will get 12-month free with limited usage after initial signup with AWS in this type of offer. After that, you pay standard rates after your 12 months free usage term expires, or your application use exceeds the free tier limits.

Trials

In this type of offer, you will get short-term free trial, which starts from the date, you activate a particular service. Then, you pay standard rates after the trial period expires.

Free Tier Eligible label

One obvious question that comes to mind when you are new to AWS is how you would know if the service you are trying to use if it is in Free Tier or not. The next question is whether it is Always Free type, 12 Months Free type, or Trials type. Some other common questions related to AWS Free Tier are at the end of this document as FAQ.

In general, if you use AWS Management Console (other options are using AWS API and AWS CLI), AWS provides some label if it is in Free Tier.

Figure 10.26 choose an instance type

For example, as you can see in the screenshot above, choosing instance type when launching an EC2 instance. There is a label "Free tier eligible" on the t2.micro instance with one vCPU and 1 GiB memory. So, if you launch an EC2 example using this instance type, it is Free Tier eligible.

AWS Free Tier Details Page

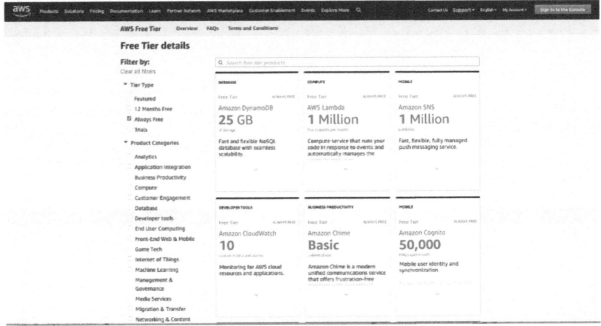

Figure 10.27 AWS Free Tier details page

Another way is: on the AWS Free Tier page https://aws.amazon.com/free, on the left side, there is a Filter by option. Using this option, you can find detail such as which services are available as Always Free, which are available as 12 Months Free, which are on Trials. So, for example, in the screenshot above, Always Free is checked, displaying the services available as Always Free. You can also filter by Product Categories such as Analytics, Database.

Summary
- AWS Free Tier enables its customers to acquire practical knowledge about AWS platform and services by reducing the cost of learning.
- They of are three types: Always Free, Short-Term Free Trial, and 12 Months Free.
- http://aws.amazon.com/free page can be used to find more details about AWS Free Tier.

FAQ

These are some FAQs from the Google search (https://www.google.co/search)

How do I know if I have AWS free tier?

To get started, **simply navigate to the Billing and Cost Management Dashboard to view the "Free Tier Usage" data**. For details on Free Tier-eligible services and how to qualify as a Free Tier-eligible customer, please refer to the AWS Free Tier page. Aug 12, 2015

Is AWS free tier really free? ⌃

The AWS Free Tier is designed to give you hands-on **experience with a range of AWS services at no charge**. For example, you can explore AWS as a platform for your business by setting up a test website with a server, alarms, and database.

Which service is chargeable in the free tier? ⌃

Hourly usage in the AWS Free Tier. Some services, such as **Amazon EC2**, Amazon RDS, and Elastic Load Balancing, charge for usage on an hourly basis. The AWS Free Tier for these services provides you with a monthly allotment of hours for the first 12 months.

What happens after AWS free tier? ⌃

When your Free Tier period with AWS expires, **you can continue to use the same services**. However, all resources on your account are billed at On-Demand rates. ... If you don't want to incur charges, you must delete, stop, or terminate the resources on your account. If you want, you can then close your account. Nov 4, 2020

Does AWS free tier expire after 12 months? ⌃

12 Months Free – These tier offers include 12 months free usage following your initial sign-up date to AWS. ... Always Free – These **free tier offers do not expire** and are available to all AWS customers.

Why is AWS charging me for free tier? ⌃

When using AWS Free Tier, you might incur charges due to the following reasons: **You exceeded the monthly free tier usage limits of one or more services**. You're using an AWS service, such as Amazon Aurora, that doesn't offer free tier benefits. Your free tier period expired. Sep 25, 2020

AWS Billing & Cost Management Dashboard

Figure 10.28 AWS billing & cost management

It is very important to have good understanding about this topic as sometimes you might have heard the saying "nothing comes free in this world."

Budget Alarm Set Up

Before using AWS, one of the critical tasks is setting up a budget alarm to help keep your AWS bills within the check.

AWS has a Free Tier; then why do I need to set up a budget alarm?

Typically for preparing AWS certification exam, it's good practice to use the services given in the AWS Free Tier. AWS Free Tier is a feature provided by AWS to try out and learn AWS services free of cost for some time, typically for one year. However, the free tier will not be sufficient to learn and try out the services if you are seriously preparing for the AWS Solutions Architect exam. For example, my AWS bill for preparing certification was around $15.

So, by setting up the budget alarm, you make sure to get some sort of notification such as email or text, depending on what you have configured if you're exceeding the budget threshold. The budget alarm will help in keeping your AWS bills within your budget. That being said, let's go ahead to set up the budget alarm.

Step 1: Billing Dashboard

In the search bar, type billing to easily find the "Billing & Cost Management Dashboard." Or, if you have previously visited this service, it will be shown on your front page once you logged in.

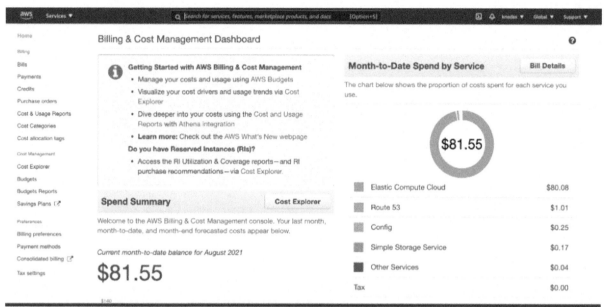

Figure 10.29 billing dashboard

Step 2: Create Budget

Once you are on the "Billing & Cost Management Dashboard" page, here click on the Budget link on the left sidebar. You will get the Overview page.

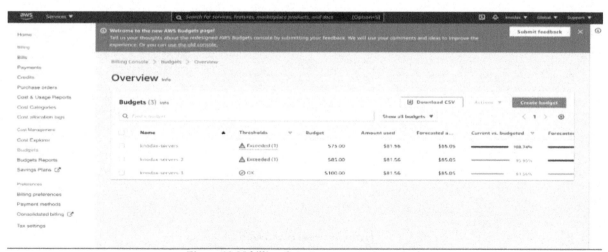

Figure 10.30 billing & cost management -- overview

On the Overview page, click on the Create Budget button which is at the top right side. It will take you to the "Choose budget type" page. Select a budget type, which is cost budget.

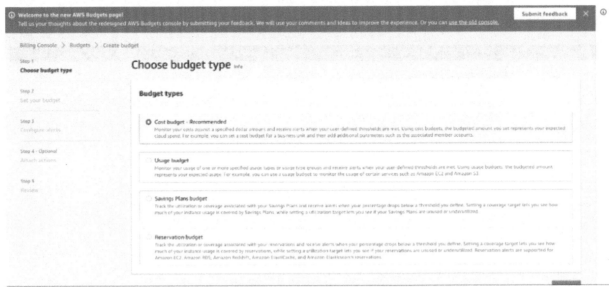

Figure 10.31 choose budget type

Step 3: Set your budget

Click next, and for the period, select monthly; and select recurring for the budget effective date. Set the starting month, and then enter the budget amount, for example, $1.00. Enter budget name, for example, "AWS Certification Preparation Budget," and then click Next.

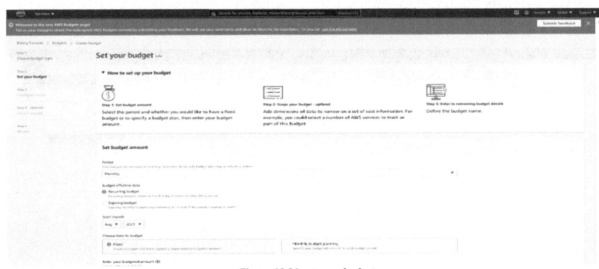

Figure 10.31 set your budget

On the next screen, enter threshold -- 80% is typical. Next, enter the email where you would like to get the notification. Please make sure you provide the correct email address. Finally, click on the create budget, and your AWS budget will be created.

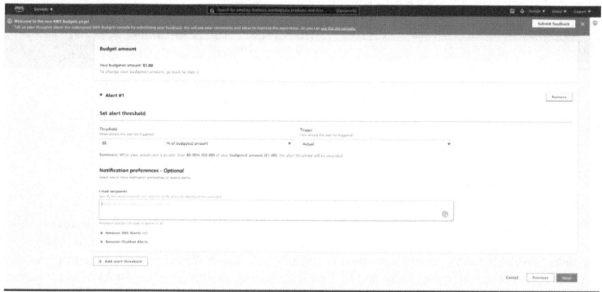
Figure 10.32 budget amount

So, with this budget setup, you will get an email notification if your bill exceeds the threshold you have set up.

How to Access AWS

AWS Management Console is a common and popular choice to access AWS as it is a compelling UI. We can perform many AWS operations on the AWS platform without programming or knowing its low-level APIs. However, AWS can be accessed in other ways as well.

Different Ways to Access AWS
- AWS Management Console
- AWS CLI -- AWS Command Line Interface
- AWS SDK -- AWS Software Development Kit
- IDE

AWS Management Console

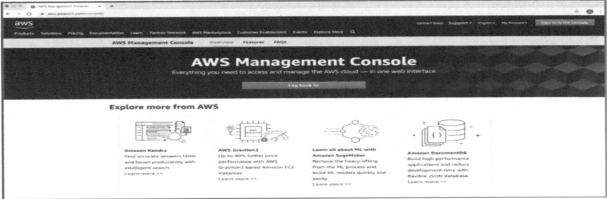

Figure 10.33 AWS management console

AWS Management Console, a more formal name for AWS UI, is a prevalent choice to access AWS. You don't need to know any programming language or scripting language to access AWS if you are using AWS its management console. You can access the AWS UI from mobile apps as well. For example, you can manage launched EC2 instances from mobile apps using AWS Management Console.

AWS CLI

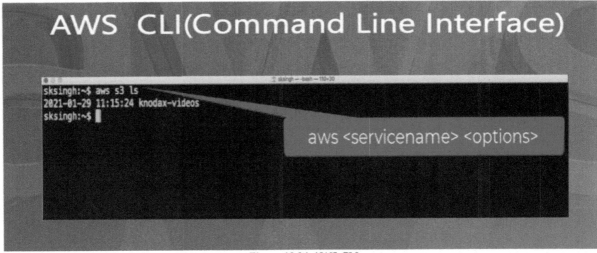

Figure 10.34 AWS CLI

The other way to access AWS is using AWS CLI, which is AWS Command Line Interface. AWS CLI is handy for DevOps engineers, who would like to access AWS from the command line to be more productive or to automate backend processes, such as launching or terminating AWS services without using its management console

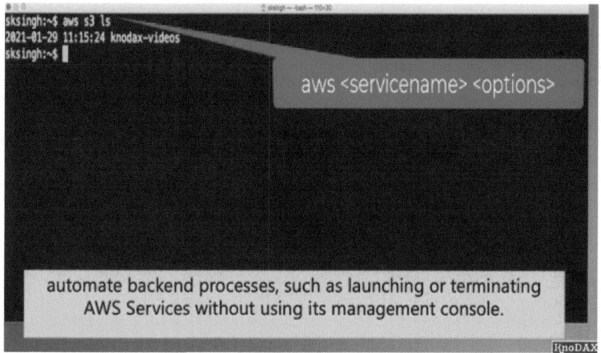

Figure 10.35 AWS CLI demo

AWS SDK

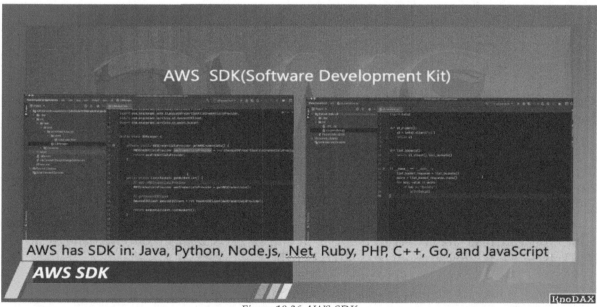

Figure 10.36 AWS SDK

The other option is AWS SDK, which is AWS Software Development Kit. The AWS SDK is used mainly by AWS Developers. AWS SDK is handy for AWS developers who would like to develop programs on the AWS platform using AWS APIs. For example, if you would like to develop a chat application on AWS. You could leverage AWS SDK in that case.

AWS has SDK in almost all mainstream programming languages. It has SDK in Java, Python, Node.js, .Net, Ruby, PHP, C++, Go, and JavaScript.

Language-specific Integrated Development Environments (IDE)
You can also use IDE. An integrated development environment (IDE) provides a set of coding productivity tools such as a source code editor, a debugger, and build tools. Cloud9 IDE is an offering from AWS under IDEs.

Related YouTube Videos

AWS Account Sign Up: https://youtu.be/RY3ldyFTYl8
AWS Free Tier: https://youtu.be/Vi4UzvkPpzE
AWS Root Account Best Practices: https://youtu.be/9OEYJGKRMJc
AWS MFA Set Up: https://youtu.be/LrFOO9Hw46c
How to Access AWS: https://youtu.be/ZX6E6RIhP7k
AWS Billing & Cost Management: https://youtu.be/bux-i6QZUe8

Chapter Review Questions

Exercise

1. Sign up for an AWS Account.
Hint: You can follow the YouTube video: https://youtu.be/RY3ldyFTYl8

2. Set up MFA for your AWS Account using Google Authenticator.
Hint: You can follow the YouTube video: https://youtu.be/LrFOO9Hw46c

3. Set up a budget alarm of $1.00 for your AWS account. This is just to learn how to set up a budget alarm. You can set as minimum as possible, for example, $0.01.
Hint: You can follow the YouTube video: https://youtu.be/bux-i6QZUe8

4. List three points about AWS Free Tier that you think are very useful to you as an AWS learner.
Hint: You can read about AWS Free Tier at https://aws.amazon.com/free and watch the YouTube video at https://youtu.be/Vi4UzvkPpzE

For the questions given below, please mark them if they are true or false.

6. AWS Basic Support is free, and it offers all AWS customers access to AWS Resource Center, Product FAQs, and Discussion Forums. True / False
7. Typically for preparing AWS certification exam or learning AWS, it's good practice to use the services given in the AWS Free Tier. Nonetheless, before using AWS, one of the critical tasks is setting up a budget alarm. True / False

8. AWS Free Tier is a feature provided by AWS to try out and learn AWS services free of cost for some time, typically for one year. True / False

Please select the correct answer from the given choices for the questions below.

9. Which of the following mechanisms can be used to add MFA in AWS?

    a. Virtual MFA Device
    b. U2F (Universal 2 Factor) Security Key
    b. Hardware MFA Device
    b. all of them

10. Which of the following ways can AWS platform be accessed?
    a. AWS Management Console
    b. AWS CLI -- AWS Command Line Interface
    c. AWS SDK -- AWS Software Development Kit
    d. all of them

11. In which of the following programming languages does AWS have SDK?
    a. Ruby
    b. Java
    c. Go
    d. all of them

Chapter 11. AWS Global Cloud Infrastructure

The AWS Global Cloud Infrastructure is the most secure, extensive, and reliable cloud platform, offering over 200 fully featured services from data centers globally. Whether you need to deploy your application workloads across the globe in a single click, or you want to build and deploy specific applications closer to your end-users with single-digit millisecond latency, AWS provides you the cloud infrastructure where and when you need it.

We know that AWS is a public cloud service provider and provides on-demand availability of all kinds of cloud services from across the world. How is AWS able to provide on-demand availability of all types of cloud services from across the globe? Well, AWS has a massive amount of computing resources and storage available in data centers spread across all over the world. The AWS entire infrastructure setup of data centers across all over the globe is called AWS Global Cloud Infrastructure. In this chapter, we will learn about AWS Global Cloud Infrastructure and its related concepts, such as AWS Availability Zones and AWS Regions.

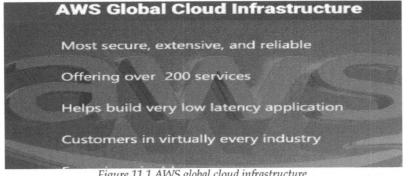

Figure 11.1 AWS global cloud infrastructure

AWS Global Cloud Infrastructure is the backbone of AWS. The AWS Global Cloud Infrastructure is the most secure, extensive, and reliable cloud platform, offering over 200 fully featured services from data centers globally. It not only allows you to deploy your application across the globe with a single click, but it also allows you to build and deploy specific applications closer to your end-users with single-digit millisecond latency. It helps millions of active customers from virtually every industry build and run every imaginable use case on AWS.

This was a high-level overview of AWS Global Cloud Infrastructure. Next, we will look into AWS Regions and AWS Availability Zones, which are other important concepts related to AWS Global Cloud Infrastructure.

AWS Regions

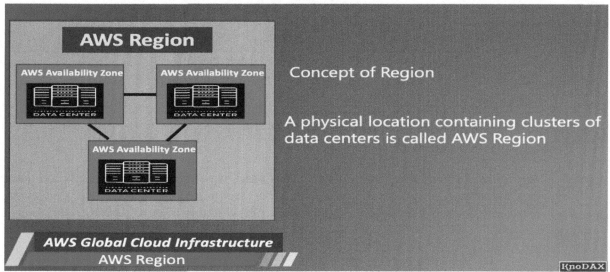

Figure 11.2 AWS Regions overview

AWS has the concept of a Region, a physical location worldwide where AWS has clusters of data centers. AWS region is a physical location that has clusters of data centers. As you can see in the picture above, the AWS Region has 3 three clusters of data centers. And these clusters of data centers are connected. Each AWS region is a separate geographical region. Each AWS region is completely independent having its own internal private secured network and is isolated from the other AWS regions.

AWS Regions on the Management Console

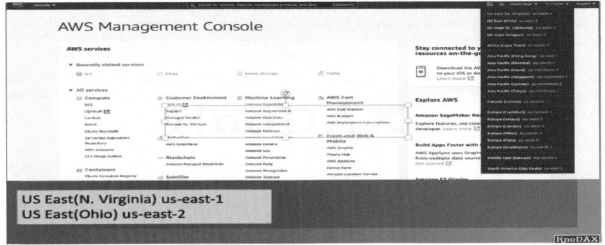

Figure 11.3 AWS Regions on management console

AWS region is displayed at the top right on the AWS Management Console. When you logged in to your AWS account, you will be assigned a default region. That way when you launch any AWS service, it will be served from that AWS region.

Each AWS region is assigned a region code, which is used in various configuration when using AWS services and resources. For example, US East (N. Virginia) AWS Region has a region code us-east-1. If a particular service you are looking for is not available in your default AWS region, you can change it.

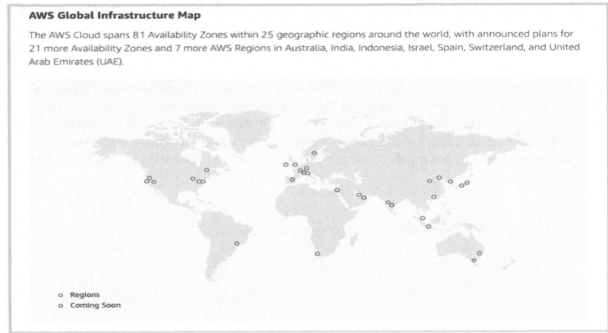

Figure 11.4 AWS global infrastructure map

Let's try to understand AWS regions by looking at the AWS Global Infrastructure Map. On the AWS Global Infrastructure map above, AWS regions are represented with circles. The blue circle ones are the current AWS regions, and AWS Regions in red circles are coming soon.

As you can see, AWS has regions all over the world. As of this writing, AWS has 25 geographic regions around the world. Seven more AWS Regions in Australia, India, Indonesia, Israel, Spain, Switzerland, and United Arab Emirates (UAE) are coming soon. With regards to AWS regions in USA, there are 6 AWS regions in USA. Two AWS regions are on the US east coast: one is in Northern Virginia, and the other is in Ohio. Two AWS regions are on the US West Coast: one is in Oregon, and the other one is in Northern California. Additionally, there are 2 Gov cloud regions: one is on US East Coast, and other is on US West Coast. Some regions have more services than others. For example. US East (N. Virginia), US West (N. California) in America; Singapore, Sydney, Tokyo in Asia Pacific; Frankfurt, Ireland in EU offer more services in general.

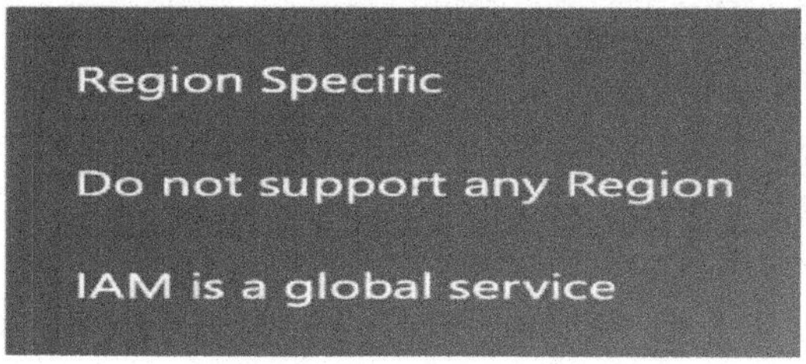

Region Specific

Do not support any Region

IAM is a global service

Figure 11.5 AWS Regions features

AWS services are region specific. However, just to keep in mind there are some services which do not support any region. For example, AWS IAM is a global service and is not associated with any region.

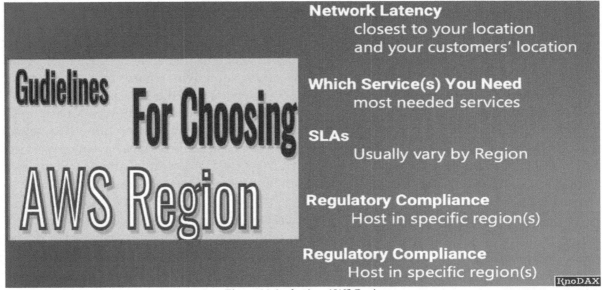

Figure 11.6 selecting AWS Region

Following are the guidelines for choosing AWS regions to help ensure excellent performance and resilience:

- To get low latency performance, choose a region closest to your location, and your customers' location to get low network latency.

- Find out what are your most needed services. Usually, the new services start on a few main regions such as regions on us-east and us-west before being available to other regions.

- Some regions will cost more than others, so use built-in AWS calculator to do rough cost estimates to get idea about your choices.

- SLAs usually vary by region, so be sure to be aware of what your needs are and if they're being met.

- You may need to meet regulatory compliance such as GDPR by hosting your deployment in a specific region or regions to be compliant.

AWS Availability Zones

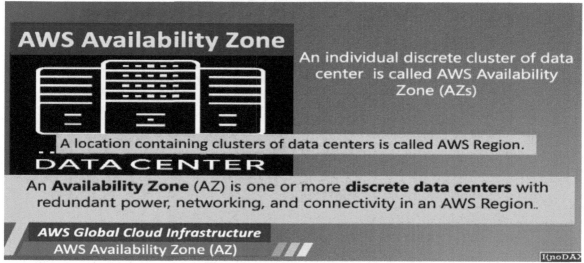

Figure 11.7 AWS Availability Zones

Another essential concept in AWS is AWS Availability Zone. It is also called AZ, in short. As I mentioned earlier, AWS has clusters of data centers on multiple locations worldwide, and a location containing clusters of data centers is called AWS Region.

On the other hand, an individual discrete cluster of the data center is called AWS Availability Zone.

Another way to way to understand is: An availability zone (AZ) is one or more discrete data centers with redundant power, networking, and connectivity in an AWS region.

LET'S SIMPLIFY AWS REGIONS AND AWS AVAILABILITY ZONES CONCEPTS

Let's simplify a bit. In an AWS region, there are clusters of data centers spread across the location. An individual discrete cluster of data center or a discrete data center is called AWS Availability Zone.

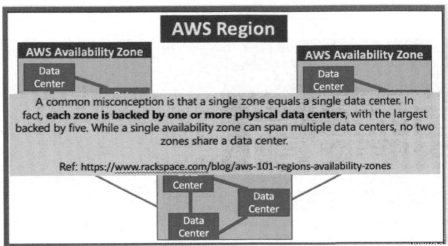

Figure 11.8 understanding AWS Regions

AWS availability zones within a region have connectivity with one another. To strengthen the concept further, I would like to share this point:

> A common misconception is that a single zone equals a single data center. Each zone is backed by one or more physical data centers, with the largest backed by five. While a single availability zone can span multiple data centers, no two zones share a data center. (https://www.rackspace.com/blog/aws-101-regions-availability-zones)

More Details About AWS Availability Zones

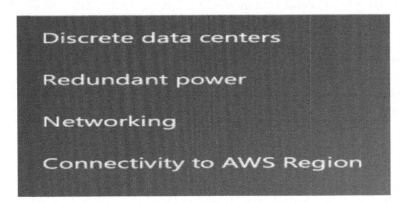

Figure 11.9 AWS Availability Zones details

Now you got a conceptual understanding of AWS Availability Zones. Let's go through some more details. Availability zones are separated in an AWS region. Availability zones are located away from the city and are in lower-risk flood areas to avoid the flood or any other kind of damage to the data centers. AZs are physically separated by a significant distance, many kilometers, from any other AZ.

An availability zone (AZ) is one or more discrete data centers with redundant power, networking, and connectivity in an AWS Region. All AZs in an AWS Region are interconnected with high-bandwidth and low-latency networking between AZs.

Own power supply

Onsite backup generator

Connected via different grid

Figure 11.10 AWS Availability Zones details

Each availability zone has its power supply and on-site backup generator. Furthermore, they are connected via different grids from independent utilities to avoid a single point of failure for any power outage.

Availability zones have code as well, like AWS regions. Availability zone code has region code + a letter added in the end. For instance, The US Ohio AWS region has region code us-east-2. And this AWS region has 3 availability zones with their code as us-east-2a, us-east-2b, and us-east-2c. If you notice, a letter has been added at the end of the region code (us-east-2+a = us-east-2a) to get the AZ code.

Availability Zones from Architectural Perspective

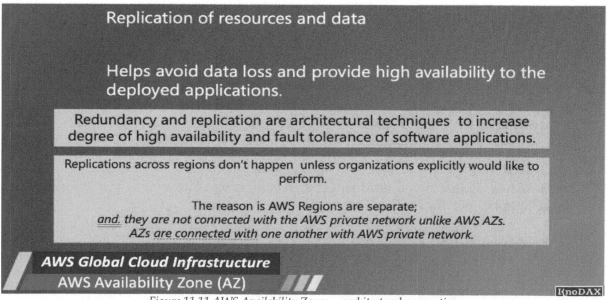

Replication of resources and data

Helps avoid data loss and provide high availability to the deployed applications.

Redundancy and replication are architectural techniques to increase degree of high availability and fault tolerance of software applications.

Replications across regions don't happen unless organizations explicitly would like to perform.

The reason is AWS Regions are separate; *and,* they are not connected with the AWS private network unlike AWS AZs. *AZs are connected with one another with AWS private network.*

AWS Global Cloud Infrastructure
AWS Availability Zone (AZ)

KnoDAX

Figure 11.11 AWS Availability Zones -- architectural perspective

Let's understand Availability Zones from the solution architecture perspective. Redundancy and replication are architectural techniques to increase the high availability and fault tolerance of software applications.

To provide redundancy, AWS allows replication of resources and data in multiple availability zones, which helps avoid data loss and offers high availability for the deployed applications. All traffic between AZs is encrypted. Furthermore, you can perform synchronous replication between AZs. However, replications across AWS regions don't happen unless organizations explicitly would like to do perform. The reason is AWS regions are separate, and they are not connected with the AWS private network, unlike AWS availability zones that are connected.

AWS Local Zones

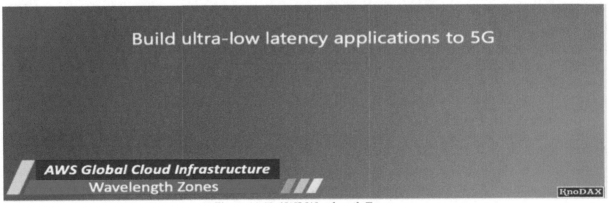

Figure 11.12 AWS Local Zones

Another concept related to AWS Global Cloud Infrastructure is AWS Local Zones. As per the AWS Local Zones documentation (https://aws.amazon.com/about-aws/global-infrastructure/localzones/):

> *AWS Local Zones are a type of AWS infrastructure deployment that places AWS compute, storage, database, and other select services close to large population, industry, and IT centers. With AWS Local Zones, you can easily run applications that need single-digit millisecond latency closer to end-users in a specific geography. AWS Local Zones are ideal for use cases such as media & entertainment content creation, real-time gaming, live video streaming, and machine learning inference.*

The key takeaway is that if you need single-digit millisecond latency closer to end-users in a specific geography, look for AWS local zones.

AWS Wavelength Zones

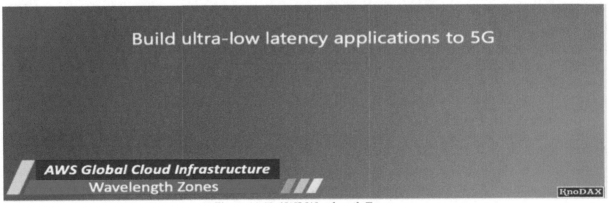

Figure 11.13 AWS Wavelength Zones

The other one is AWS Wavelength, an AWS infrastructure offering optimized for mobile edge computing applications. As per the AWS Wavelength Zones documentation (https://aws.amazon.com/wavelength/)

AWS Wavelength is an AWS Infrastructure offering optimized for mobile edge computing applications. Wavelength Zones are AWS infrastructure deployments that embed AWS compute and storage services within communications service providers' (CSP) data centers at the edge of the 5G network, so application traffic from 5G devices can reach application servers running in Wavelength Zones without leaving the telecommunications network. This avoids the latency that would result from application traffic having to traverse multiple hops across the Internet to reach their destination, enabling customers to take full advantage of the latency and bandwidth benefits offered by modern 5G networks.

The key takeaway is if you are deploying applications to leverage 5G, look for AWS wavelength.

Related YouTube Videos

AWS Global Infrastructure: https://youtu.be/FeGbJK5l3zc
AWS Regions: https://youtu.be/Jd45yh_GbR8
AWS Availability Zones: https://youtu.be/8kNZ_Ko91Os

Chapter Review Questions

Exercise

1. Find out what is your AWS Account's default AWS Region? Then, choose any of your favorite AWS services from the Search bar on the AWS Management Console.

2. Note down your AWS Account's default AWS Region. Change your AWS Account's default AWS Region to any other AWS Region in another country. Do you notice any change -- can you find the AWS Service you chose in question 1?

3. Choose IAM Service. Find out if it is associated to any AWS Region.

4. Find out the AWS Services that are global -- means they are not associated with any AWS Region.

5. Change your AWS Account's default Region to what you noted down in the question 2.
Hint: You can find the YouTube video: https://youtu.be/Jd45yh_GbR8 helpful

For the questions given below, please mark them if they are true or false.

6. AWS Region is a physical location that has clusters of data centers. True / False

7. An Availability Zone (AZ) is one or more discrete data centers with redundant power, networking, and connectivity in an AWS Region. True / False

8. With AWS Local Zones, you can easily run applications that need single-digit millisecond latency closer to end-users in a specific geography. True / False

9. AWS Wavelength is an AWS infrastructure deployment that embeds AWS compute and storage services within communications service providers' data centers at the edge of the 5G network, so applications traffic from 5G devices can reach application servers running in Wavelength Zones without leaving the telecommunication network. True / False

10. Each AWS Region is completely independent having its own internal private secured network and is isolated from the other AWS Regions. True / False

11. Each AWS Region is assigned a region code, which is used in the various configurations when using AWS services and resources. True / False

12. Most AWS services are region-specific. True / False

13. AWS IAM is a global service and is not associated with any AWS Region. True / False

14. To get low latency performance, choose an AWS region closest to your location, and your customers' location to get low network latency. True / False

15. Some regions will cost more than others, so use a built-in AWS calculator to do rough cost estimates to get an idea about your choices. True / False

16. You may need to meet regulatory compliance such as GDPR by hosting your deployment in a specific region to be compliant. True / False

17. All AZs in an AWS Region are interconnected with high-bandwidth and low-latency networking between AZs. True / False

18. To provide redundancy, AWS allows replication of resources and data in multiple Availability Zones, which helps avoid data loss and offers high availability for the deployed applications. True / False

19. All traffic between AZs is unencrypted. True / False

20. You can perform synchronous replication between AZs. True / False

21. Replications across AWS regions don't happen unless organizations explicitly would like to do perform. The reason is AWS regions are separate, and they are not connected with the AWS private network, unlike AWS availability zones that are connected. True / False

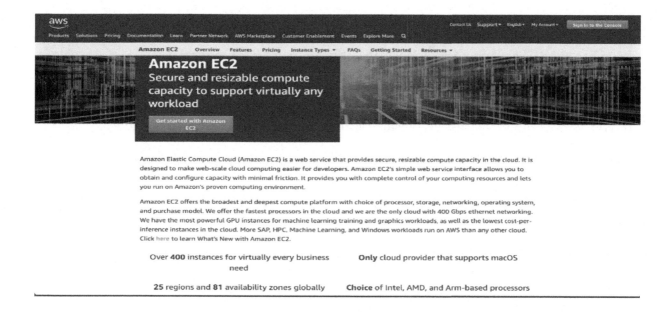

Amazon Elastic Compute Cloud (Amazon EC2) is a web service that provides secure, resizable compute capacity in the cloud. It is designed to make web-scale cloud computing easier for developers. Amazon EC2's simple web service interface allows you to obtain and configure capacity with minimal friction. It provides you with complete control of your computing resources and lets you run on Amazon's proven computing environment.

Amazon EC2 offers the broadest and deepest compute platform with choice of processor, storage, networking, operating system, and purchase model. We offer the fastest processors in the cloud and we are the only cloud with 400 Gbps ethernet networking. We have the most powerful GPU instances for machine learning training and graphics workloads, as well as the lowest cost-per-inference instances in the cloud. More SAP, HPC, Machine Learning, and Windows workloads run on AWS than any other cloud. Click here to learn What's New with Amazon EC2.

Over **400** instances for virtually every business need   **Only** cloud provider that supports macOS

25 regions and **81** availability zones globally   **Choice** of Intel, AMD, and Arm-based processors

Chapter 12. Elastic Compute Cloud (EC2) Introduction

Introduction

We know that AWS is a public cloud service provider and provides on-demand availability of all kinds of cloud services from across the world. Being a public cloud service provider, it offers different types of services, categorized into different types of cloud computing. For example, in the Cloud Computing Platform Types chapter, you learned that IaaS, PaaS, SaaS are the main cloud computing platform types. Virtual servers are one of the primary examples of IaaS cloud computing type, and EC2 (Elastic Compute Cloud) is AWS IaaS type of cloud computing type. In other words, using EC2, you can get the infrastructure as a service, such as virtual servers. Using EC2, we can launch Linux, Windows, macOS types of virtual servers. In this chapter, we will learn about Elastic Compute Cloud (EC2). First, we will understand EC2 theoretically, and later we will learn how to launch Ubuntu Linux virtual server using the EC2 service and understand various aspects of EC2. We will also learn how to ssh into the launched Linux virtual server.

EC2 is a very old AWS service to launch virtual servers on AWS. Now, let's understand what EC2 does: "It is a web service that provides secure, resizable compute capacity in the cloud." In this statement, let's parse some keywords or phrases to understand EC2 better.

Web Service
The first is web service. What it means is that you can access an EC2 instance using an HTTP endpoint.

Secure
The other important word in this statement is secure. What it means is that you can control inbound and outbound traffic to an EC2 instance.

Resizable Compute Capacity

The other important phrase is resizable compute capacity. What it means is that EC2 instances have an auto-scaling feature. Using an auto-scaling feature, you can let EC2 instances scale up or down based on various metrics such as CPU utilization or I/O throughput.

Cloud
The last word is cloud. What it means is that EC2 instances are launched in AWS data centers. Or in AWS terms, we can say that EC2 instances are launched in AWS availability zones.

On this EC2 web page, we would like to bring your attention to these four points.

Over **400** instances for virtually every business need   **Only** cloud provider that supports macOS

25 regions and **81** availability zones globally   **Choice** of Intel, AMD, and Arm-based processors

- You can launch four hundred different types of EC2 instances.
- AWS is the only cloud provider that supports macOS.
- You can launch ec2 instances in 25 regions and 80 availability zones globally.
- You have a choice of different types of processors.

EC2 Instance, Web Server, and ssh

We have got a high-level introduction of EC2. Let's understand how to launch an EC2 instance, set up an Apache Web Server on the EC2 instance. And finally, how to do ssh connection to a launched EC2 instance. This is a typical hands-on example of learning EC2.

Let's log in to the AWS management console.

AWS Management Console

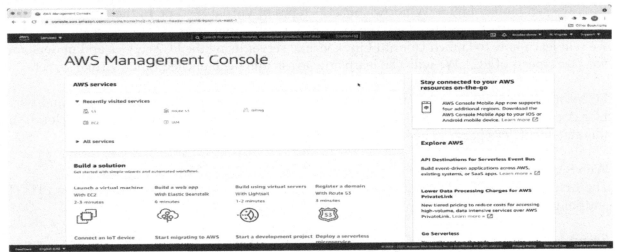

Figure 12.1 AWS Management Console

EC2 Service Home Page

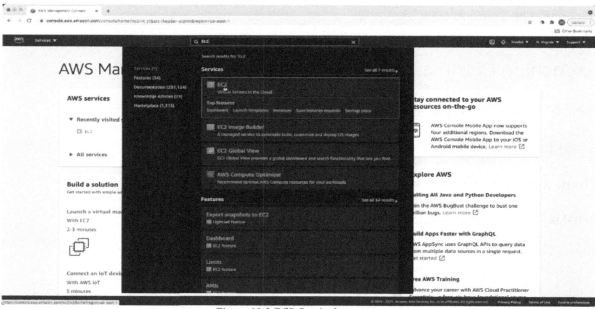

Figure 12.2 EC2 Service home page

Go to EC2 service either by typing "EC2" on the search bar or selecting EC2 from recently visited services if it is shown.

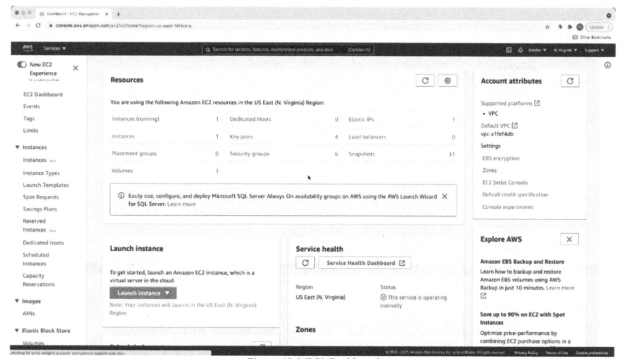

Figure 12.3 EC2 Dashboard

This is the EC2 Dashboard. As you can see in my account, one instance is already running. At the top right, you will see your account name. The next is your default AWS region. In my case, it is N. Virginia, which has AWS region code us-east-1. In your case, it could be different depending on your location.

Launching EC2 Instance

Since we will be launching an instance, click on the Launch Instance button.

Step 1: Choose Amazon Machine Image (AMI)

The next step is to choose AMI, which is Amazon Machine Image.

What is AMI or Amazon Machine Image?

Amazon Machine Image or AMI is a template of software configuration. So, for example, AMI of Red Hat Linux will have software configuration to the launched Red Hat Linux instance running as a virtual server in the cloud.

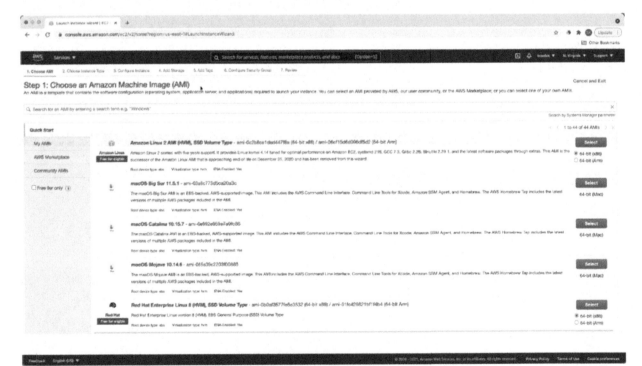

Figure 12.4 choose AMI

Default all AMIs are listed. You can search for Linux, Windows, Mac AMIs.

Windows AMIs

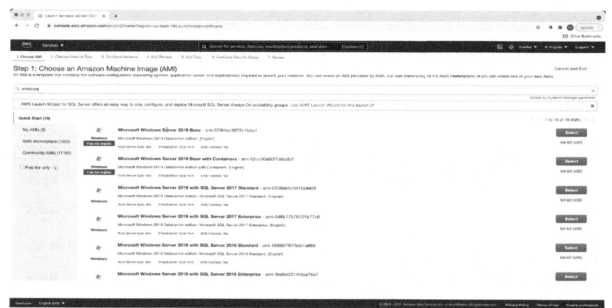

Figure 12.5 search for Windows AMIs

Let's search for "Windows" to find out Windows AMIs. Here in the search results, you get all the Windows AMIs. So, if you are looking to launch Windows virtual machine on AWS, you can choose among these AMIs depending on what exactly you are looking for on Windows.

macOS AMIs

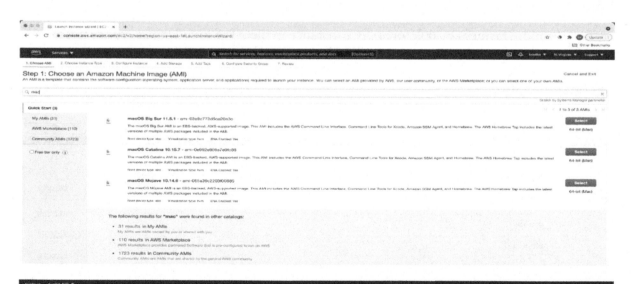

Figure 12.6 search for macOS AMIs

You can launch macOS EC2 instance as well. Let's search for "mac" in the search area. You get three macOS AMIs.

Linux AMIs

Figure 12.7 search for Linux AMIs

Since we will be launching a web server on a Linux EC2 instance, let's search for Linux. We will get many choices in the result, which one should we select?

AWS Free Tier

The first deciding factor is to look for an EC2 instance in the AWS Free Tier, as we are not looking for a high-end configuration. Just minimal RAM and Hard Disk are OK.

Amazon Linux AMI

Figure 12.8 search for Amazon Linux AMI

Since we are launching a Linux virtual machine on AWS, the next deciding factor is to look for an Amazon Linux AMI, which will have pre-installed AWS-related binaries.

Cloud Computing and AWS Introduction

159

AWS CLI (Command Line Interface)

Usually, it's a good idea to use an Amazon Linux AMI because you get some additional features related to AWS already set up. For instance, if you need to run AWS CLI commands on the launched EC2 instance, you don't need to install AWS CLI separately. That's the reason we will select Amazon Linux 2 AMI, which is Free Tier eligible, and the default 64-bit x86 is good. So, let's select Amazon Linux 2 AMI.

Step 2: Choose Instance Type

Here, select t2.micro as it is Free Tier eligible. The t2.micro is an instance type.

What is Instance Type?

AWS has EC2 instance categorization based on combinations of CPU, memory, storage, and networking capacity. The t2.micro is one of the instance types.

There are other instance types, such as t2.small, t2.medium, t2.large, and t2.xlarge. They all have a varying degree of memory, storage, and networking capacity. In other words, different instance types have different CPU, memory, storage, and networking capacity.

Step 3: Configure Instance Details

Figure 12.9 configure instance details

Here, default is OK. The only thing we will add here is we will add a couple of Linux shell commands in the User data section to install the webserver.

User data

You can specify user data to configure an instance or run a configuration script during launch. The one advantage of User Data is if you launch more than one instance at a time, the user data is available to all the instances in that reservation.

The user data to set up a web server on the EC2 instance is given below:

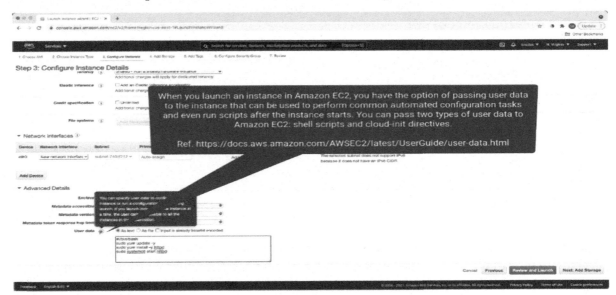

Figure 12.10 EC2 configure instance -- user data

In this, the first line is about using the bash shell. The second line is to update OS – it's always good practice to update the OS. In case if there is any security patch that has been released but is not yet available in AMI, which could lead to potential security risks. The third line is about installing an HTTP web server. And the last line starts the server. Additionally, whenever this EC2 instance stops and starts again, the httpd daemon will be started, which means the webserver will be started automatically at the server startup.

Step 4: Add Storage

Figure 12.11 EC2 instance -- add storage

The next step is to add storage. The default 8 Gb is OK.

Step 5: Add Tags

Figure 12.12 EC2 instance -- add tags

The next step is to add tags. This is optional. However, if you would want, you can add, for example, you can add "name" as a key and "Apache Web Server Test" as a value.

Step 6: Configure Security Group

Figure 12.13 configure security group

The next step is about configuring the security group.

What is a Security Group?

The security group is a mechanism to control inbound and outbound connections to the launched EC2 machine. For example, what type of traffic and sources are allowed to make the connection on the launched ec2 instance? For example, is inbound FTP connection allowed? If allowed, is it allowed from all IP addresses or selected IP addresses?

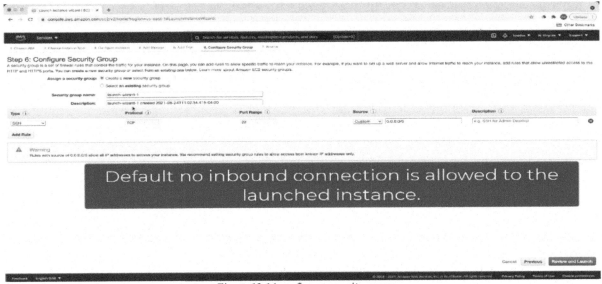

Figure 12.14 configure security group

With regards to default settings, no inbound connection is allowed to a launched EC2 instance.

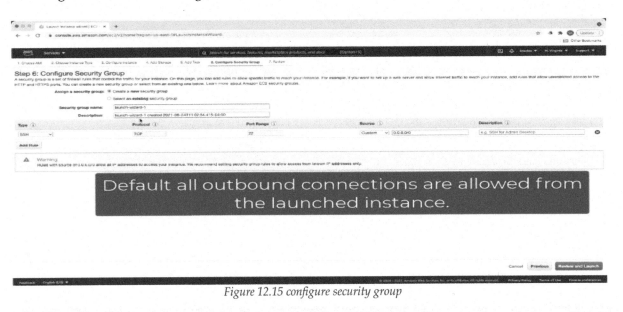

Figure 12.15 configure security group

Default, all outbound connections are allowed from a launched EC2 instance. That being the case, we need to set up inbound connections for this instance. We will create a new security group and name it: apache-web-server-test-sg. For the description, we will add "Apache web server security group to learn how to launch a web server on EC2."

Rules for Inbound Connections

Figure 12.16 rules for inbound connection

Now let's add a rule for the inbound connections. The first is, we need to open a port to make an ssh connection to the launched ec2 instance from the local Mac machine.

Change the source IP so that ssh connection can only be done from your machine only. So, change the Source to your IP. And secondly, you need to open an HTTP connection port for the webserver. Here, we will click on ADD Rule. We will select HTTP on Type. And for Source and we would like the webserver to be accessed from anywhere, so, we will change Source to Anywhere.

Step 7: Review and Launch

Now click on Review, and then Launch.

Figure 12.17 review and launch

We will create new key pair. You need key pair to make a ssh connection to the launched machine. Enter the name of the key pair for example. We will name it: ec2-web-server-test-key and download the new key pair. You will need to download the key pair. Otherwise, you will not be able to make the connection to the launched instance using your terminal.

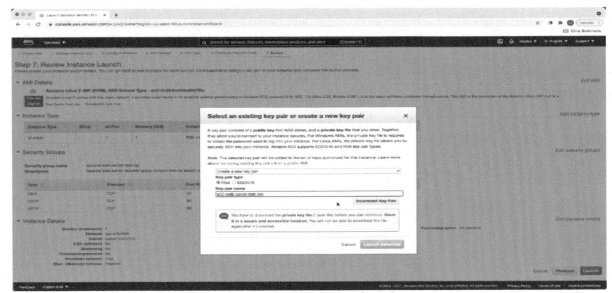

Figure 12.18 EC2 instance - key pair

Click on the Launch Instance button. It says that your instances are now launching.

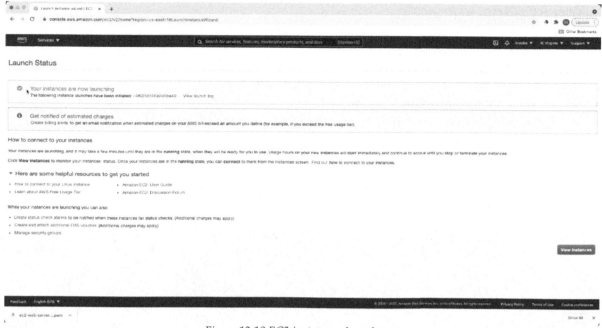

Figure 12.19 EC2 instance -- launch status

Test the Launched EC2 Instance

Let's get the public IP of the launched EC2 instance machine and open the browser to make sure if your instance is set up with an Apache web server.

A quick way to test is if your web server is installed and running is to click on the Open address. As you can notice, we got the Apache Web Server test page.

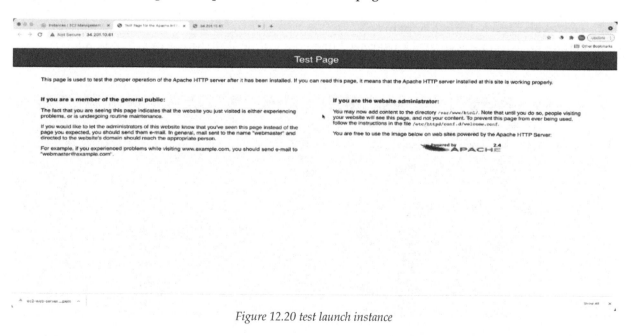

Figure 12.20 test launch instance

ssh to EC2 Instance

(In this example I'm using macOS) Now, let's learn how to use ssh connection to the EC2 instance from my local machine. Create a "temp" directory on the local Mac machine. From this directory, we will connect to launched EC2 instance using ssh. The steps are as follows:

- Let's open a Mac terminal window
- Create a temp directory on your machine and go to the temp folder.
- Copy the downloaded security key pair to this temp folder.
- Change the permission of the key file to ensure the key is not publicly viewable.

chmod 400 ec2-web-server-test-key.pem

Figure 12.21 setting permission on the key file

- Connect to the launched instance using its Public IP or DNS.

For example:
ssh -i ec2-web-server-demo-key.pem ec2-user@ec2-18-205-160-41.compute-1.amazonaws.com
The syntax is "ssh -I key name ec2-user@ec2 instance Public IP Address or DNS name."
The default username for the Amazon Linux EC2 instance is ec2-user.

Figure 12.22 ssh to the launched EC2 instance

Let's go to the directory where the web server is installed: /var/www/html.
And create a test.html file. Just add a line "this a web server test page."

Figure 12.23 sample test.html file

Test the webserver, by adding http://<Public IP Address>/test.html in the URL

 As you can notice, test.html is displayed in the browser.

Figure 12.24 output of test.html

Connect to EC2 From AWS Management Console

You can also connect to an EC2 instance from the AWS Management console.

Figure 12.25 list of running EC2 instance

Stop, Reboot, or Terminate

You can stop, reboot, or terminate a launched EC2 instance.

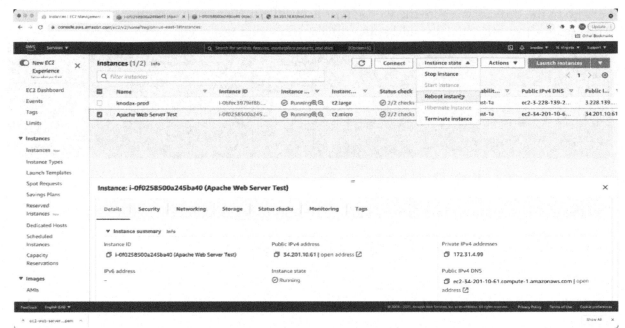

Figure 12.26 stop, reboot, or terminate EC2 instance

It's a good practice to terminate an instance if you don't need it -- as on AWS we typically pay based on the usage: pay-as-you-go pricing model.

Related YouTube Video

Introduction to EC2: https://youtu.be/amYSuat4Bh4

Chapter Review Questions

Exercise

1. Launch an EC2 instance of Amazon Linux AMI using Free Tier. In other words, there should not be any charge for the EC2 instance that you will launch in this exercise. When launching the instance, make sure only two inbound ports are open: ssh and HTTP. Making ssh connections is only allowed from your local machine. The HTTP port connection is open from anywhere. Download the security key and keep it in a safe place. On the EC2 instance page, make sure that instance status is displayed as "running." Use default settings if it is not mentioned in the question or you are unsure about your input.

URL showing different statuses of EC2 instance:
https://docs.aws.amazon.com/AWSEC2/latest/UserGuide/ec2-instance-lifecycle.html
Note down the public and private IP addresses of the launched EC2 instance. Note down the name of the Security Group.

2. If the instance is running as per question 1, connect to the launched EC2 instance from your machine using an ssh connection. You may have to change the permission of the downloaded key.

3. Once you are connected to the launched instance, as per question 2, install Apache Web Server on the launched EC2 instance, and start the Apache Web Server.

4. Test the Apache Web Server you set up in question 3 by accessing it from your local machine's Web Browser. Use the public IP address of the launched EC2 instance to test the Apache Web Server. Did you get the Apache Web Server's Home Page you set up on your launched EC2 instance? If the answer is Yes, then your Apache Web Server setup is correct.

5. Terminate the launched EC2 instance.
Hint: Use YouTube Video: https://youtu.be/amYSuat4Bh4 to complete the exercise questions.

For the questions given below, please mark them if they are true or false.

6. EC2 is a web service that provides secure, resizable compute capacity in the cloud. True / False

7. You can launch a macOS type of virtual server on AWS. True / False

8. You have a choice of different types of processors when launching EC2 instances. True / False

9. When you logged in, AWS Management Console displays your default AWS Region. Can you change your default AWS Region in the AWS Management Console? True / False

10. The AMI of Red Hat Linux will have software configuration to the launched Red Hat Linux instance running as a virtual server in the cloud. True / False

11. One of the reasons for choosing Amazon Linux AMI is that Amazon Linux AMI has pre-installed AWS-related binaries such as AWS CLI. True / False

12. The different EC2 instance types have different CPU, memory, storage, and networking capacity. True / False

13. You can specify user data to configure an instance or run a configuration script during launch. The one advantage of User Data is if you launch more than one instance at a time, the user data is available to all the instances in that reservation. True / False

14. The security group is a mechanism to control inbound and outbound connections to the launched EC2 instance. True / False

15. All inbound connections are allowed to a launched EC2 instance. This is the default setting. True / False

16. To open inbound connections, for example, an HTTP connection, for a launched EC2 instance, you will have to add a rule in the security group for the EC2 instance. True / False

17. The default username for the Amazon Linux EC2 instance is ec2-user. True / False
P

Please select the correct answer from the given choices for the questions below.

18. Which of the following options is an EC2 instance type?
      a. t2.micro
      b. t2.xlarge
      b. t2.large
      d. all of them

19. When you download the key pair of the launched EC2 instance, you will need to restrict the permission of the security key file(.pem) in order to use the key for ssh connections. Which of the following options is the correct command to change the permission of a key file?
      a. chmod 600 <keyfile name>
      b. chmod 750 <keyfile name>
      c. chmod 400 <keyfile name>
      d. chmod 777 <keyfile name>

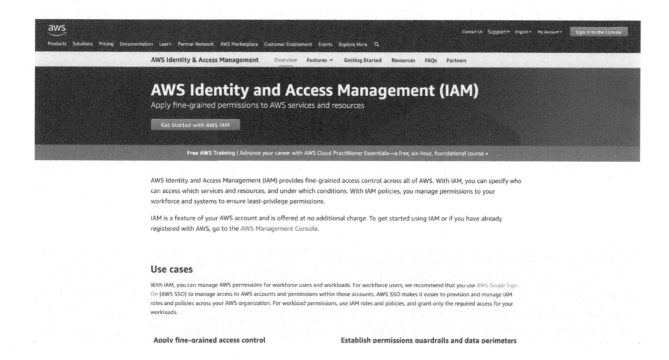

Chapter 13. Identity and Access Management (IAM) Introduction

It is an essential chapter with regards to the AWS foundational concept. First, we will get the theoretical understanding of Identity and Access Management (IAM), IAM users and groups, IAM Policy, and then create an IAM user. Let's first start with what IAM is.

Introduction to Identity and Access Management (IAM)

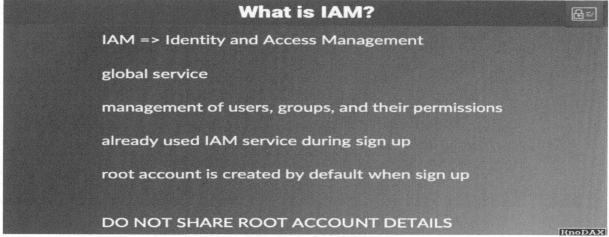

Figure 13.1 what is IAM

IAM is the abbreviated form of Identity and Access Management. It is a global service, which means it is not associated with any AWS region -- most AWS services have a region scope. However, a handful of them has global scope -- IAM has global scope. It deals with the management of users, groups, and their permissions. In other words, using the IAM service, we can create users and groups and assign them permissions means what the users and groups can do on that AWS account.

You already used the IAM service when you signed up for AWS. When you sign up for AWS, an AWS root account is created. AWS root account is created default when you sign up for AWS. You should use your AWS root account in very rare situation. In fact, you should create another user, and use that user account instead of the root user account. And do not share your root user account user id, password, and access keys with anyone.

Now we know that IAM is used for the management of users, groups. In other words, we can create users and groups using the IAM service.
Let's understand the IAM users and groups concept. Before going into details, I just wanted to clarify that you might hear both AWS and IAM users. Both are the same. Depending on the context, one is generally used over the other. AWS user is a more general term; however, we use the term IAM user when referring specifically to the context of IAM. Semantically both terms are the same.

You should create separate IAM users for each person in your organization. In other words, an AWS account/person in your organization. However, it's good practice to create a group for the users if they do similar operations. Why? Because that way, if you need to add additional permission, just add that permission to the group, and it will be assigned to all group users. On the same token, if you remove permission from the group, it will be removed for all group users.

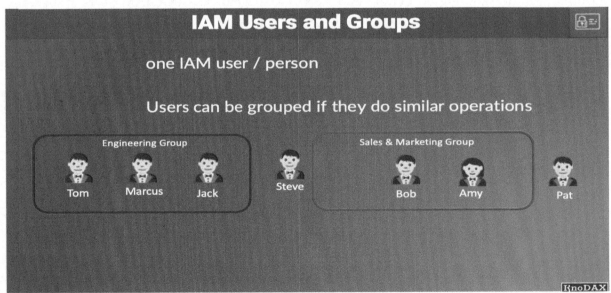

Figure 13.2 IAM users and groups

Let's try to understand the AWS users and groups concepts. Suppose we have a startup organization with seven employees. Tom, Marcus, and Jack are in the Engineering group; Bob and Amy are in the Sales & Marketing group; Pat is in Finance, and Steve is CEO.

In this scenario, we will have to create 7 IAM users -- one for each employee. Since Tom, Marcus, and Jack are in the engineer's group, we will need to create an Engineering group and add them to the engineering group.

Since Bob and Amy are in Sales & Marketing, we will create a Sales & Marketing group and add Bob and Amy to the Sales & Marketing. Now Steve is CEO. Being CEO, sometimes, he helps the Engineering group, and sometimes he allows the Sales & Marketing group. So, we will add Steve to both groups. Pat will be in no group as he takes care of the Finance department alone until he extends his fiancé group to add more employees.

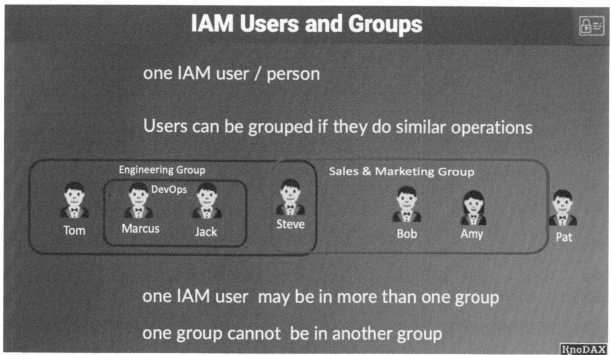

Figure 13.3 IAM users and groups

As you can see, an AWS user could be in more than one group. For example, suppose you later created a DevOps group and if Marcus and Jack are part of the DevOps group. Then, you can add Marcus and Jack into the DevOps Group. So, we got the idea, we need one IAM user per person, and users could belong to a group if they perform similar operations. One IAM user may be in more than one group, which is generally good, making user management easier. You cannot have one group in another group.

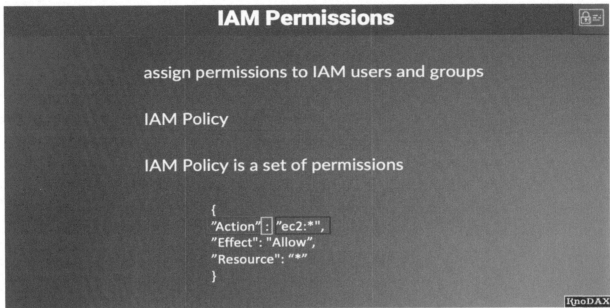

Figure 13.4 IAM policy

Now how will we allow AWS users and groups to use AWS? To enable users or groups, to do what they are allowed to do, we will have to assign permissions. How will we assign permissions? Well, there is a concept of IAM policy, which contains a set of permissions.

IAM policy is written in JSON as you can see in the screenshot. JSON is easy to understand. It is structured written in a key-value format separate as a colon. For example, the JSON statement in

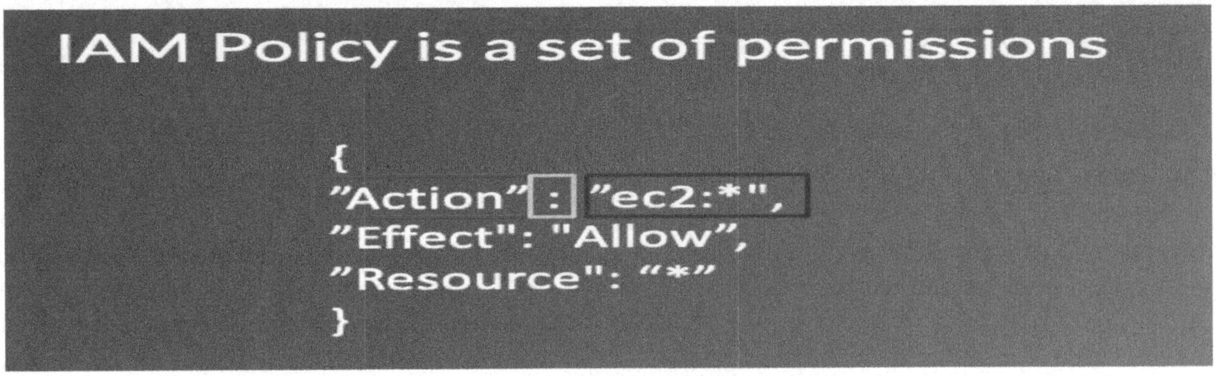

IAM Policy is a set of permissions

```
{
"Action" : "ec2:*",
"Effect": "Allow",
"Resource": "*"
}
```

Figure 13.5 IAM policy

permission is assigned to an IAM user or group, the user or group can perform any EC2 operation on any resource.

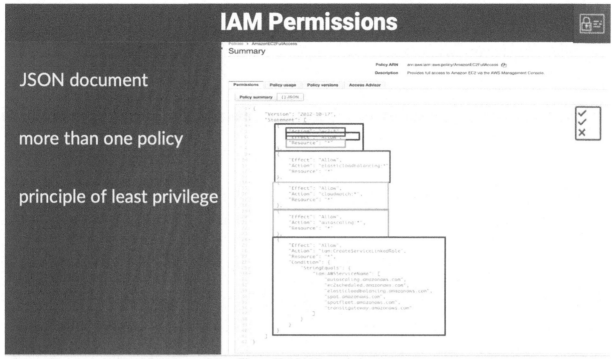

Figure 13.6 IAM permissions

The main point to understand here you assign permissions to an IAM user or a group using the IAM policy. IAM policy is a set of permissions, as you can see in the document. The individual lines, which are also called statements, are given within the curly brackets. So, for example, you have one set of permissions for EC2 and another set for elasticloadbalancing and so on. For each permission set, you provide action that you are considering, Effect which could Allow or Deny, and on which resource or resources you would want the defined action to be applied upon.

If we assign this policy to any user or group, then that user or group will perform operations based on the approach. An IAM user or group cannot do anything unless a policy is assigned. More than one policy can be assigned to a user or group.

You should not assign more permissions than a user needs it. The is called the principle of least privilege, which helps in your overall AWS account security. If you didn't follow this principle, you could have situations where users could be doing or trying out something, for example, launching hundreds of EC2 instances, and organizations would get surprised charges on the AWS bill. Additionally, there could be potential security-related issues as well.
Now we will learn how to create an IAM user.

Create IAM User (Hands-on)

Let's log in to the AWS management console.

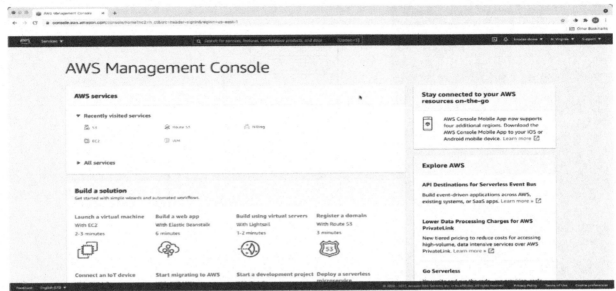

Figure 13.7 AWS Management Console

I'm logged in, and I'm on the AWS Management Console page.

Search for IAM Service

Since I need to add IAM User, I need IAM service, which is Identity and Access Management service. A quick way to find the service is to type the service name in the Search area. Or you can find it from the recently visited services panel.

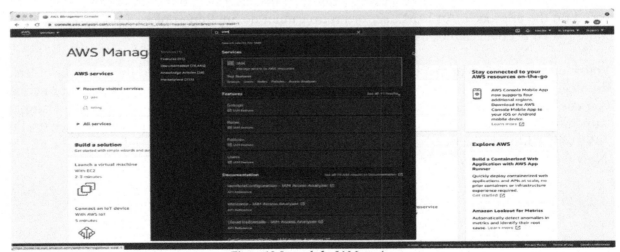

Figure 13.8 search for IAM service

Cloud Computing and AWS Introduction   177

Since I would like to show you how to search for services, I'll use the search bar. I'll Type here IAM in the search area. Then, I'll click on IAM. I will get the IAM service home page.

IAM Service Console

Figure 13.9 IAM service console

Whenever you need to create an AWS user, you will use the IAM service. In the beginning, some terms may be confusing, but as you do more learning of AWS, you will feel very comfortable with these terms.

IAM Users Page

For example, AWS user or AWS IAM user is the same thing. Click on Users; I already have a couple of users here.

Figure 13.10 IAM users

Click on Add Users button to add a new user.

Add User

Figure 13.11 IAM add user

Enter username – I'll enter John Doe. This is just a demo user to show you how to add an IAM user to AWS. Next is the Select AWS Access type. I'll check both checkboxes.

The first one is for programmatic access. Checking this option will also generate and enable an access key ID and secret access key. These keys are needed to interact with AWS programmatically using AWS API, CLI, SDK, and other development tools. For example, you will need these keys if you use AWS CLI, AWS Command Line interface. AWS CLI is used mainly by AWS DevOps engineers.

These keys are also needed if you are using AWS SDK, which is AWS Software Development Kit. AWS SDK is used mainly by AWS developers who are building software using AWS APIs. The main point here is that if you are adding a new user and if this user will have an AWS Developer or DevOps type of role, have the programmatic access option checked.

And the other one is for the AWS Management Console Access. This is a typical and common way to access AWS, and most AWS users are comfortable with this option, so it is ok to have this option checked in most situations. So let me check this option.

The next option is about the console password, which will be used to log into the AWS Management Console. Please note, when using AWS API, you will be using your account access keys, which are AWS Access Key and AWS Secret Key. I'll have this option checked. If you are an admin and create a user for someone else, usually you will use an autogenerated password; and have this option checked. You can also add a custom password – it means not an auto-generated one.

Next is Require password reset check box. I'll leave it as it is -- it means checked. That way, AWS will force to create a new password at the next sign-in. Click on the Next button, which is about permission.

Attach Policy

Figure 13.12 IAM attach policy

Here click on "Attach existing policies directly" and select "AdministratorAccess" policy so that this new user will have admin privilege to this account.

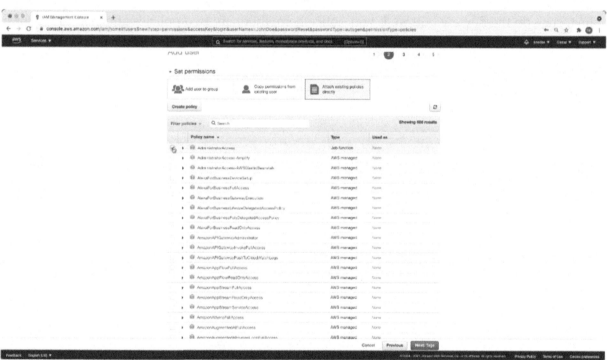

Figure 13.13 attach existing IAM policy

AWS has many existing policies which you can directly attach to an IAM user.

Tag

Click on tags; I'm not creating any label for this user, as this is optional.

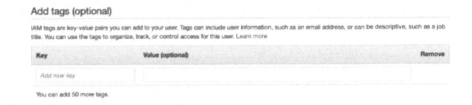

Figure 13.14 IAM user creation -- add tags

However, you can add here user email address, job title as a tag.

Review

Next, click on the Review button. If you notice here, there are two policies attached to this user. One is AdministratorAccess, and the other one is IAMUserChangePassword.

Figure 13.15 IAM user creation -- review

The IAMUserChangePassword policy is added as we chose the option for auto-generated passwords.

Create User

Next, click on Create User button. Now the user is created.

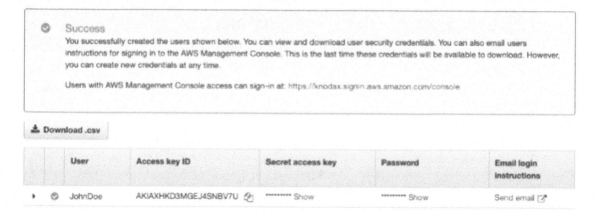

Figure 13.16 IAM user creation confirmation

As you can see, since I have selected programmatic access, Access Key ID, Secret Access Key is generated. Furthermore, since I selected the option for the auto-generated password, the user Password is generated as well. I'll not note down the password and download access keys.

Since I selected AWS Management Console access, the newly created user will also get an AWS Management Console URL to log in to the AWS management console.

Let me copy this URL and Password.

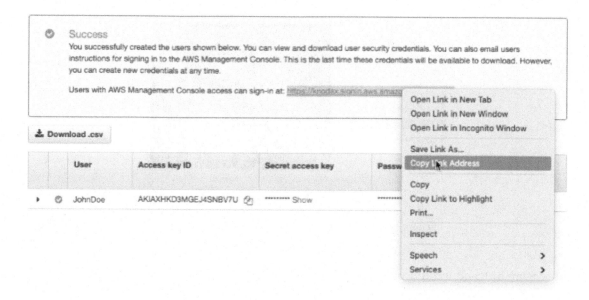

Figure 13.17 getting sign in URL of the new IAM user

The user has been created.

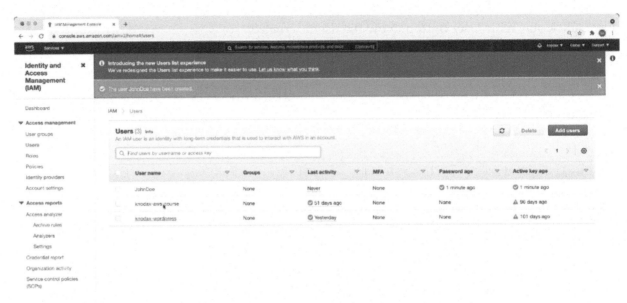

Figure 13.18 newly created IAM user is listed

Test the Created User

Let's test if it works. First, I'll open a new window. Here enter the current password and new password.

Figure 13.19 AWS log in using newly created IAM user

Since it was an auto-generated password, it is asking to change the password.

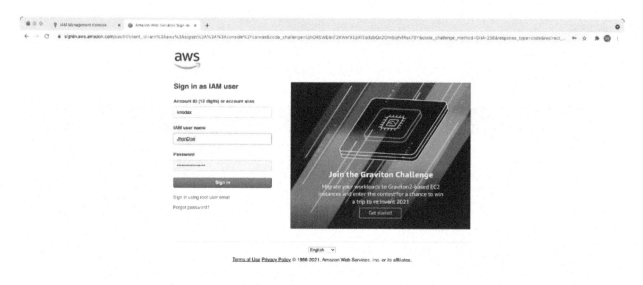

Figure 13.20 IAM user change password

I'll create a new password and click on Confirm password change button. As you can see, I'm logged using this newly created IAM user, which is JohnDoe.

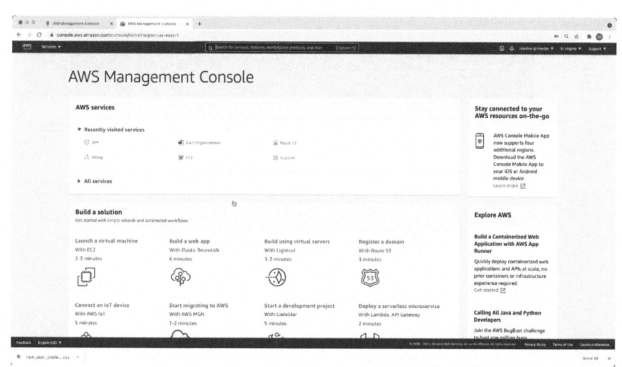

Figure 13.21 AWS management console of logged in IAM user

Delete User

If you would like to delete this user, go to the IAM Service home page. Then, click on the user and click Delete user.

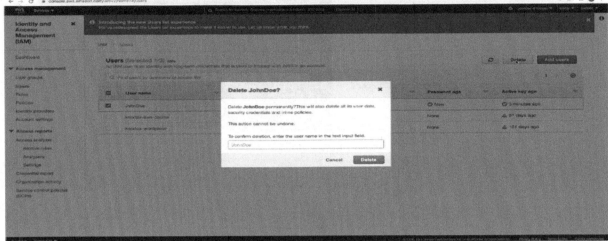

Figure 13.22 delete user confirmation

And the user is deleted.

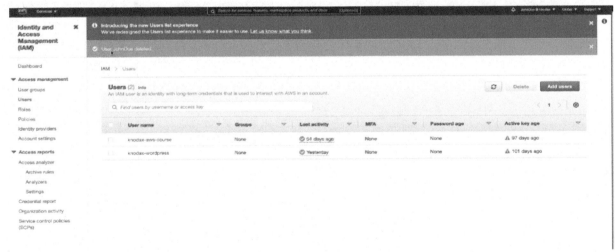

Figure 13.23 user deleted -- not listed

Related YouTube Video
Introduction to IAM: https://youtu.be/_8_twt71xTY

Chapter Review Questions

Exercise

1. Create an IAM User John Doe in your AWS Account. Make this user an administrator of your AWS Account. Test by logging in with this newly created admin user to make sure it works.

2. Delete the user created in question 1 from your AWS Account.

3. Create three IAM users in your AWS Account: Rich Smith, John Doe Sr., Bob Thomson. Next, create a group called "DevOps" in your AWS Account. Add users: Rich Smith, John Doe Sr., Bob Thomson into the DevOps Account.

4. Assign the DevOps group permissions to act as administrator for EC2 and S3 services.
Hint: You can watch the YouTube video: https://youtu.be/_8_twt71xTY to get help on the exercise questions.

For the questions given below, please mark them if they are true or false.

5. When creating an IAM user, you will need to generate an access key ID and secret access key if you would like to provide programmatic access using AWS API, CLI, SDK, and other development tools to the created IAM user. True / False

6. IAM policy is a set of permissions. True / False

Please select the correct answer from the given choices for the questions below.

7. Which of the following AWS services is used to create IAM users?

      a. AWS Lambda
      b. API Gateway
      c. IAM
      d. EC2

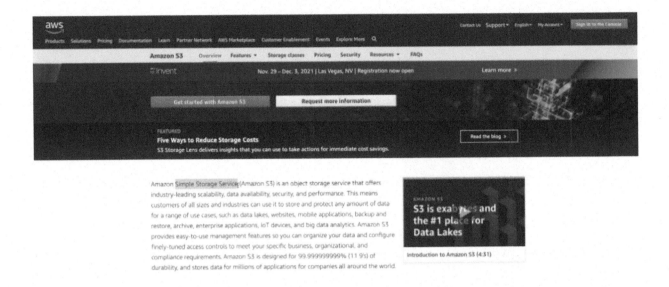

Chapter 14. Simple Storage Service (S3) Introduction

As we know that IaaS is one of the main cloud computing types. In IaaS, cloud providers, provide infrastructure such as virtual servers, virtual storage services over the Internet. You already learned EC2 which is AWS IaaS cloud computing type of service to launch virtual servers on the cloud. Like EC2, S3 (Simple Storage Service) is also an AWS IaaS cloud computing type of service. S3 provides a virtual storage service on the AWS cloud platform. In the chapter, we learn about the introduction to S3 and do hands-on to upload an image on S3.

What is Simple Storage Service (S3)?

S3 (Simple Storage Service) is a very old and popular AWS service. Essentially, S3 is a cloud storage service of AWS. The first noticeable point about S3 is that it is object storage built to store and retrieve any amount of data from anywhere. S3 provides a set of APIs to store and retrieve data on the cloud. A few terms such as object storage, scalability, data availability, security, performance, compliance, and durability are essential to understand S3 to have an excellent conceptual understanding of what S3 is. Let's first understand about object storage system as S3 is an object storage service.

Object Storage System

S3 is an Object Storage Service

Let's understand the phrase object storage because this is the key to understanding S3. Regarding storage, I guess we are more familiar with file storage, which is a type of storage system used by operating systems. However, S3 is not a file storage service – it is an object storage service – this is a crucial concept to keep in mind.

Objects are the Distinct Units

The question, then, is: what is object storage or object-based storage? In object storage, objects are the distinct units to manage and manipulate data storage. Or, in more simple words, data storage is managed as objects.

No Folder or Hierarchy Concept

In object storage, there is no folder or hierarchy concept like we have in file storage systems. Instead, in an object storage system, everything is stored in a flat address space, which is also known as storage pool. In AWS, this storage pool has a particular name – called "bucket."

Metadata

Another essential point about object storage is metadata. Metadata about objects are attached with stored objects, which is one of the reasons that we can do high performant analytics on AWS.

That's the reason even though we don't have any idea about objects' content, still, because metadata is attached to objects, we can query objects.

Object Storage Systems can be Scaled Out

Another feature of an object storage system is that object storage systems can be scaled out. This is the key reason the S3 storage system has virtually unlimited scalability.

The question is, what is the term scale-out in a storage system?

Types of Storage Systems

There are two types of storage systems: classic scale-up storage that most of us are familiar with as it is used in file-based storage systems. The other one is scale-out which is closely related to object storage systems.

Classic Scale-up Storage
In a scale-up system, the storage scalability is limited by how many maximum disks can be attached to storage controllers -- you cannot add more storage if the machine has reached the limit of how many maximum disks can be attached.

Scale-out System
On the other hand, with a scale-out system, you have a cluster of machines forming a storage address space called storage pool or Bucket in AWS terms. To increase storage capacity, just add more machines, which makes scale-out systems virtually unlimited scalable.

Object storage characteristics, such as storing objects in flat address space, metadata, and scale-out are the critical factors in driving S3 features.

S3 Features

Object Storage System

Since S3 is an object storage system, and object storage systems have virtually unlimited scalability, as we talked earlier, that being the case, S3 has theoretically virtual unlimited scalability, which is a sort of logical conclusion.

5tb is the Max Size of an Object on S3

Each object is stored in a bucket, and there is a limitation for the maximum size of the object which can be stored in a S3 bucket. The limit is 5TB what it means you cannot upload an object larger than 5TB on S3.

Fully Qualified Domain Name

Each S3 bucket gets a fully qualified domain name, and you use the fully qualified domain of a bucket to access objects in a S3 bucket.

Data Availability

S3 replicates data or content of the S3 Bucket in a minimum of three availability zones within a selected region.

Since availability zones are physically separate, the replication of data on the additional availability zones helps increase the degree of availability if there is any device failure or facility issue at the data center of an availability zone. For instance, since data are replicated on two additional AZs, data can be sustained even though data are lost concurrently in two facilities.

Security

S3 provides many securities-related features. For instance, you can store data in an encrypted form using different types of encryption mechanisms.

Performance

In S3, you can store data in a region nearest to your location. That way, you will get low latency, which leads to better performance.

Compliance

S3 has the feature of cross-region replication, which can manage regulatory compliance or keep a copy of data in case of a region failure.

Durability

Another final keyword here that I would like to bring your attention to is durability. S3 has 11 9's (99.999999999) durability, which means if you store 100 billion objects in S3, you will lose one object at most.

Summary

To summarize, S3 is an object storage service that offers scalability, data availability, security, and performance, and durability of 11 9's. Additionally, you can manage regulatory compliance as well using cross-region replication.

S3 Bucket and Upload Object to S3

Let's do a hands-on exercise of creating an S3 bucket uploading a file on S3.

Let's log in to the AWS Management Console.

AWS Management Console

Now I'm logged in, and I'm on the AWS Management Console page.

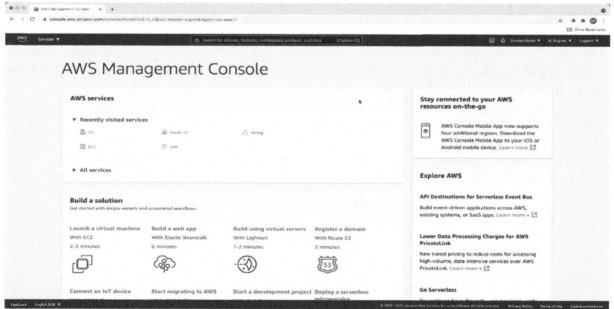

Figure 14.1 AWS management console

S3 Home Page

Now, go to the S3 service home page.

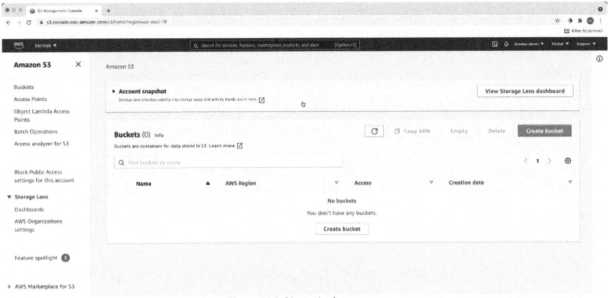

Figure 14.2 S3 service home page

I would like to bring your attention to the top right corner. The first is the account name. You will see your account name here.

Then, the next placeholder is for AWS Region. Since S3 is a global service, it doesn't show any specific region – it says global. I'm on this page to upload an image. But I don't see any option to upload the image.

Here comes an interesting point that is related to the object storage concept. Since S3 is object-based storage, we need to create a storage pool to store objects. This storage pool is called Bucket.

We first need to create a bucket to upload the image, because currently there is no bucket listed in my account.

Click on Create bucket button.

Create S3 Bucket

Now I'm on the Create Bucket page. First, I need to enter the bucket name. Let's talk about bucket names– bucket names must be unique within a partition.

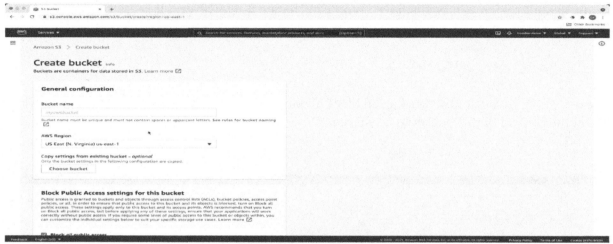

Figure 14.3 create S3 bucket

S3 Bucket Name

Bucket names must be unique within a partition. A partition is a grouping of AWS Regions. For example, AWS currently has three partitions: aws (Standard Regions), aws-cn (China Regions), and aws-us-gov (AWS GovCloud [US] Regions).

Let me give Bucket name knodax-demo-test Usually, it's a good technique to use a domain name in a bucket name, which usually avoids the possibility of name collision.

Next is AWS Region. This is where your actual data is stored.

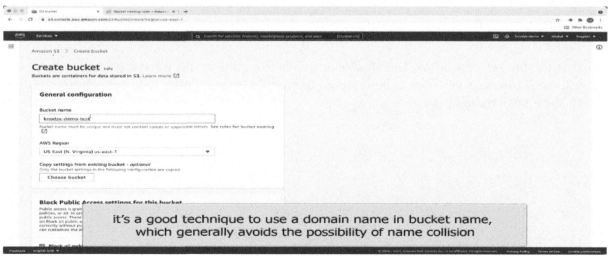

Figure 14.4 S3 bucket name

AWS Region

Select the region which is nearest to your location to have low latency and good performance.

Your default region will be displayed; you can change it. However, I'll keep it as it is, as this is my nearest region.

Public Access for Bucket

Next is public access for this bucket. I'll block all public access, as this is my private bucket. I don't want the content of this bucket to be shared.

Figure 14.5 public access for bucket

If I were using this bucket to store my website contents, I would have unchecked this box, which would have allowed public access.

S3 Bucket Versioning

Next is the bucket versioning; the *Disable* option is fine. But if you have a use case where you would want previous versions to be retained to recover from unintended user actions, you will check the enable radio button.

Figure 14.6 S3 bucket versioning

S3 Bucket Encryption

The next option is about whether you would want the content of this bucket to be encrypted. For me, Disabled is okay. I don't need to encrypt the content of this bucket – as this bucket will only have images, and encryption will be extra overhead to impact performance.

Figure 14.7 encryption setting for S3 bucket

Advanced Settings

Next is advanced settings. This is about if you don't want objects to get deleted in the bucket. Disable option is fine. I don't have any regulatory compliance sort of data in this bucket which I would like to be not deleted.

Figure 14.8 S3 bucket advanced settings

The Disable option is acceptable to delete the content of this bucket if I would like to.

Click on Create Bucket.

S3 Bucket List

As you can see that the bucket has been created. I'm on the knodax-demo-test bucket page.

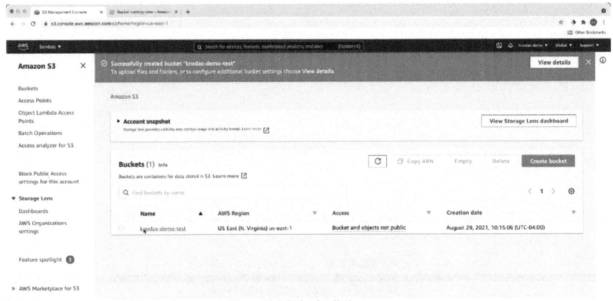

Figure 14.9 S3 bucket listing page

If you select the bucket, you can see options to delete the bucket and empty the bucket. You cannot delete a bucket if there is any object in the bucket.

Click on the Bucket. Now I'm on the bucket page.

S3 Bucket

Figure 14.10 S3 bucket page

Let me click on the upload button to upload an image that I have.

Now I'm on the Upload page.

Upload to S3 bucket

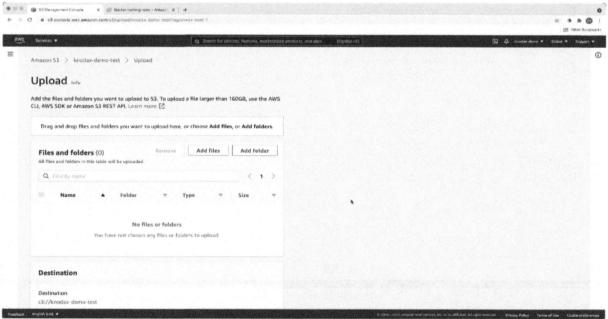

Figure 14.11 upload to S3 bucket

Click on the Add files button to upload files. You also have the option to add a folder if you would like to add your content in a folder.

Please note that creating a folder will not make it a file storage system. It will just mimic the structure of a file system -- s3 is an object storage system. The folder structure becomes key for the object, which is used to find the object

Let me click on Add files; I'll add an AWS image.

Upload Object

Figure 14.12 upload file to S3 bucket

Click on upload.

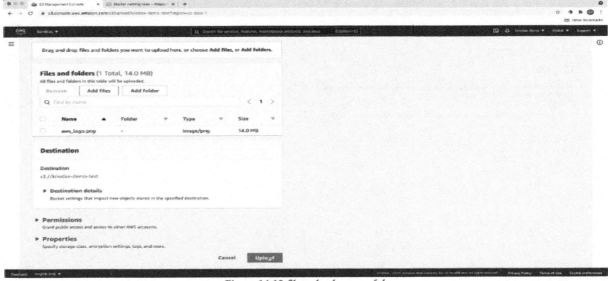

Figure 14.13 file upload successful

Now the image is getting uploaded -- upload is successful.

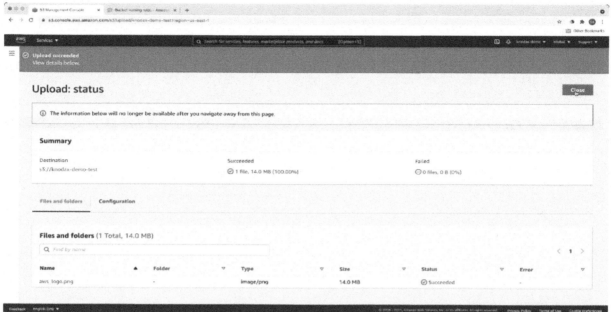

Figure 14.14 S3 bucket upload status

Click on close and view the uploaded image. Next, select the image and click on the image link.

Uploaded Object Details

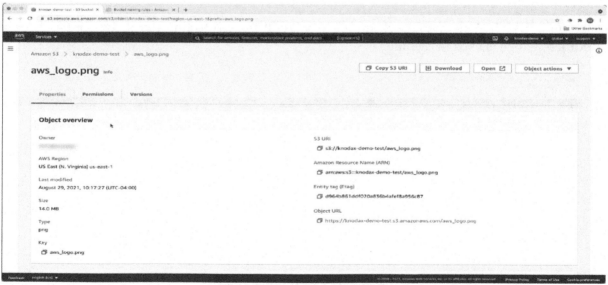

Figure 14.15 uploaded object details

On the page, details about the image are displayed, for instance, Owner, AWS Region, last modified, size, type, key, S3 URI, a unique fully qualified domain name to access the image.

You will use this URI if you write code to access the image from your Java or Python code.

ARN

Next is ARN, which is used to manage permissions on the object – for instance, ARN can be used in IAM to set access permissions about this object.

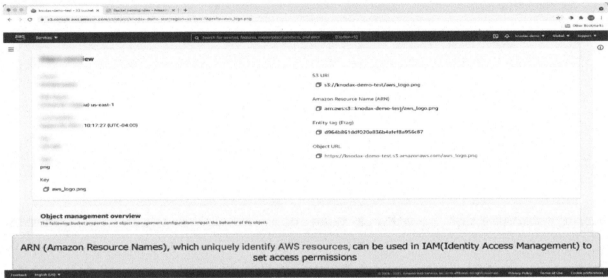

Figure 14.16 uploaded object ARN

ETag

Then Etag, which is the md5 checksum of that file. It is used to find out if the object has been modified, which is used in caching.

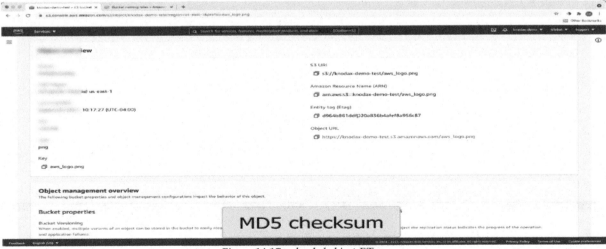

Figure 14.17 uploaded object ETag

View the Uploaded Object

Let's click on the open URL to view the image.

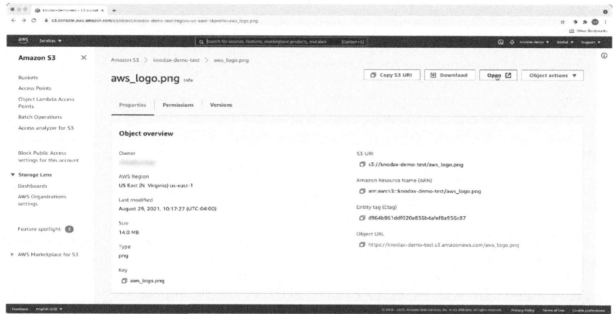

Figure 14.18 uploaded object overview

This is the AWS image that I uploaded.

Figure 14.19 uploaded object displayed on S3 console

Related YouTube Video:
Introduction to S3: https://youtu.be/JbPnpS5pXq8

Chapter Review Questions

Exercise

1. Create an S3 Bucket into your AWS Account.

Bucket names are unique in the entire AWS. The naming rules for creating S3 Bucker: Bucket names must be between 3 (min) and 63 (max) characters long. Bucket names can consist only of lowercase letters, numbers, dots (.), and hyphens (-). Bucket names must begin and end with a letter or number.

2. Upload an image into the S3 Bucket created in question 1. Retrieve the image using its URL from the browser. Download the uploaded image from the S3 Bucket.

3. Upload a document into the S3 Bucket created into question 1; make sure the document is stored as encrypted.

For the questions given below, please mark them if they are true or false.

4. In an object storage system, there is no folder or hierarchy concept like in file storage systems. Instead, in an object storage system, everything is stored in a flat address space called a storage pool. True / False

5. In an object storage system, there is no folder or hierarchy concept like in file storage systems. Instead, in an object storage system, everything is stored in a flat address space called a storage pool. True / False

6. In AWS, a storage pool is called a "bucket." True / False

7. On S3, each object is stored in a bucket, and there is a limitation for the maximum size of the object that can be stored in a bucket. The limit is 5TB which means you cannot upload an object larger than 5TB on S3. True / False

8. Each AWS bucket name must be unique as an AWS bucket name scope is global. True / False

9. Each AWS bucket gets a fully qualified domain name. True / False

10. Metadata about objects is attached to stored objects, which is one of the reasons that we can do high performant analytics on AWS. True / False

11. Object storage systems can be scaled out. This is the key reason the S3 storage system has virtually unlimited scalability. True / False

12. S3 replicates data or content of the S3 Bucket in a minimum of three AWS availability zones within a selected AWS region. True / False

13. You can store data on S3 in an encrypted form using different types of encryption mechanisms. True / False

14. In S3, you can store data in an AWS region nearest to your location. That way, you will get low latency, which leads to better performance. True / False

15. S3 has the feature of cross-region replication, which can help manage regulatory compliance or keep a copy of data in case of a region failure. True / False

Please select the correct answer from the given choices for the questions below.
16. What is the maximum size of an object on S3?
    a. 5 GB
    b. 5 MB
    b. 5 TB
    d. 5 KB

17. What is the durability of content on S3?
    a. 13 9's (99.99999999999)
    b. 9 9's (99.9999999)
    c. 7 9's (99.99999)
    d. 11 9's (99.999999999)

Chapter 15. AWS Security and Compliance

"The main element you cannot delegate to your cloud service provider is your
responsibility for security, compliance and customer trust."

— Vice President Global Chief Information Security Officer 2018 Global CISO
of the year

We live in a time when any enterprise application is like a castle that needs to be secured and
protected. Security becomes even more crucial when the application is deployed on a cloud
platform – not in your on-prem data center. In this chapter, we will discuss how the AWS cloud
platform handles security and compliance at a high level.

AWS Security

AWS cloud security is much like security in an on-premises data center.

How Important is Security?

How important is security for organizations?

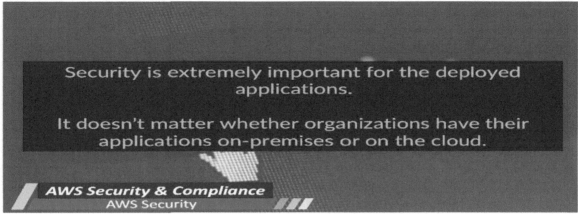
Figure 15.1 security overview brief

How important is security? It doesn't matter whether organizations have their applications on-premises or on the cloud. Security is crucial for the deployed applications.

What is Security?

What is security from an enterprise applications perspective?

Figure 15.2 what is security

Security, a core non-functional requirement in most enterprise systems. It deals with accidental leakage, theft, integrity compromise, or deletion of a valuable information asset.

How AWS Handles the Security?

How AWS handles the security of enterprise applications on its platform?

Highly Secured Data Centers

To maintain trust and confidence in their customers, AWS has implemented comprehensive security mechanisms or safeguards in place to keep customers' data safe. All data are stored in highly secured AWS data centers.

Security Architecture Keeping in Mind Requirements of Most Security-Sensitive Organizations

To continue further on how AWS approaches security to provide peace of mind to its customers. AWS has built its data centers and network architecture in such a way to meet the requirements of the most security-sensitive organizations. What it means organizations can get their security requirements with much lower operational costs.

Organizations would also inherit best practices of AWS policies, architecture, and operational processes, which were already built into the AWS core security infrastructure. That way, AWS satisfies the demand of most security-sensitive organizations.

Shared Security Model

AWS Infrastructure is designed from the cloud architectural perspective -- with the security best practices in mind. AWS shares security responsibilities with the organizations where AWS takes care of the security of the underlying infrastructure while organizations must take care of the applications' security.

Layered Security

Figure 15.3 AWS layered security

AWS uses a layered approach to security. It makes sure that underlying systems are monitored from potential threats and protected round the clock. AWS environments are continuously audited, with certifications from accreditation bodies across geographies and verticals.

What Benefits Does AWS Security Provide?

What benefits does AWS security provide to enterprise applications deployed on its platform?

In summary following are the benefits of AWS Security:

Keeps Customers' Data Safe

The AWS infrastructure puts strong safeguards in place to help protect your privacy. All data are stored in highly secure AWS data centers.

Meets Compliance Requirements

AWS manages dozens of compliance programs in its infrastructure.

Saves Cost

Customers save in cost as they would not have to manage on-premises security. The region is the security would be addressed in AWS data centers.

Scale Quickly

Security scales based on the AWS cloud usage. No matter the size of your business, the AWS infrastructure is designed to keep your data safe.

AWS Compliance

Another essential foundational concept to understand is how AWS approaches compliance. AWS helps organizations when it comes to compliance with applications deployed on its platform. Compliance requirements vary country or region-wise. When applications are deployed on AWS, organizations have complete control and ownership of their applications in that region to set up their secure, governance-focused applications. Additionally, they apply compliance and audit features.

Assurance Programs with Which AWS Complies

The following is a partial list of assurance programs with which AWS complies.

It complies with SOC1, SOC2, and SOC 3. It complies with Federal Information Security Management Act (FISMA), Department of Defense Information Assurance Certification, Accreditation Process (DIACAP), and Federal Risk and Authorization Management Program (FedRAMP).

It also complies with Payment Card Industry Data Security Standard (PCI DSS) Level 1. Finally, it complies with various ISO such as ISO 9001, 27001.

Related YouTube Video
AWS Security and Compliance: https://youtu.be/adHGVrB-j8s

Chapter Review Questions

For the questions given below, please mark them if they are true or false.

1. AWS shares security responsibilities with the organizations where AWS takes care of the security of the underlying infrastructure while organizations must take care of the applications' security. True / False

Please select the correct answer from the given choices for the questions below.

2. Which of the following compliance options does AWS Cloud Platform support?

    a. Federal Information Security Management Act (FISMA)
    b. Department of Defense Information Assurance Certification, Accreditation Process (DIACAP)
    c. Federal Risk and Authorization Management Program (FedRAMP)
    d. Payment Card Industry Data Security Standard (PCI DSS) Level 1
    e. All of them

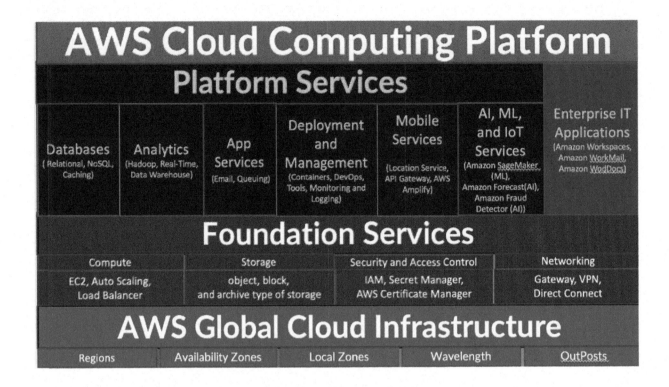

Chapter 16. AWS Cloud Computing Platform

"If you go with the platform that has the most capabilities and the right tools for the job, only makes it easier to migrate all your existing applications but also to enable your builders to build anything they can imagine."

-- *Andy Jassy, CEO Amazon*

This is the final chapter of the book. In this chapter, you will learn about the AWS cloud computing platform with respect to the categorization of some primary services. You will learn high-level overview of many popular AWS services which may help you in AWS certification exams as well.

As of 2021, AWS comprises over 200 products and services, including computing, storage, networking, database, analytics, application services, deployment, management, machine learning, mobile, developer tools, and IoT.

I have chosen a few main ones as examples to bring the main objective: how various AWS Services fit into the larger scheme of things to help understand the AWS cloud computing platform.

AWS Global Cloud Infrastructure

AWS Global Cloud Infrastructure

Regions	Availability Zones	Local Zones	Wavelength	OutPosts

Figure 16.1 AWS global cloud infrastructure

Let's start with AWS Global Cloud Infrastructure. AWS Global Cloud Infrastructure is the core foundation of AWS. In my opinion, it's challenging to imagine AWS leadership position in the cloud computing platform without AWS Global Cloud Infrastructure. AWS has data centers in multiple locations all over the world.

The clusters of data centers are called the Region, and the single cluster of data centers is known as the availability zone. In addition to availability zones, AWS Global Cloud Infrastructure has the concept of Local Zones, Wavelength, and OutPosts. These services are there to help improve the network performance of applications that have low latency requirements.

AWS Foundation Services

Foundation Services

Compute	Storage	Security and Access Control	Networking
EC2, Auto Scaling, Load Balancer	object, block, and archive type of storage	IAM, Secret Manager, AWS Certificate Manager	Gateway, VPN, Direct Connect

Figure 16.2 AWS foundational services

Then we have foundation services that leverage AWS Global infrastructure. We can classify foundation services primarily in Compute, Storage, Security and Access Control, and Networking categories at a high level.

AWS Compute

AWS has an EC2 service in the compute category, which is one of the oldest AWS services. EC2 is the abbreviated form of Elastic Compute Cloud. EC2 is used to launch virtual machines on the cloud – these launched virtual machines are called EC2 instances. So, for example, you can launch Linux, Windows, and other types of EC2 instances.

Furthermore, AWS also has an Auto Scaling service in this category, which is beneficial if you have a strong service level agreement or non-functional requirements of high availability and performance. Auto Scaling service can automatically launch instances depending on some kinds of metrics, for example, if CPU utilization is over 70% of total capacity, or Request Count Per Target, etc.

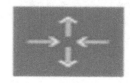

Finally, there is also an ELB service, which is Elastic Load Balancer. Usually, an Elastic load balancer is used with Auto Scaling service, which distributes incoming requests on available EC2 instances.

AWS Storage

Let's move on to the next category of foundation services, the AWS Storage category. AWS has different types of storage services. For example, AWS has S3 – Simple Storage Service -- an object storage service.

Then there is an EBS service, an Elastic Block Storage service to store block storage type. For example, when we keep files on disk, the operating system stores files in blocks.

AWS also has an archival service that is used to store files for later retrieval.

AWS Security and Access Control

Let's move on to another critical category of foundation services which is Security and Access Control. There is an IAM service in this category. IAM is the abbreviated form of Identity and Access Management. IAM Service is used to manage users, groups, and their permissions, for example, what services and resources AWS users can use or care for.

AWS also has a Secret Manager service for managing encryption keys. Furthermore, there is an AWS Certificate manager service to generate and manage SSL certificates and many more.

Networking

Another important category of foundation services is Networking. In this category, AWS has an API Gateway service, which is conceptually similar to a router. Gateway service is used to connect EC2 instances on an internal private network to the Internet.

Additionally, AWS has a service to set up a VPN to secure your on-prem network to the AWS cloud network.

And there is also a Direct Connect service with the functionally identical role as VPN, but Direct Connect is much more secure and has higher bandwidth than VPN.

Platform Services

Platform Services					
Databases (Relational, NoSQL, Caching)	Analytics (Hadoop, Real-Time, Data Warehouse)	App Services (Email, Queuing)	Deployment and Management (Containers, DevOps, Tools, Monitoring and Logging)	Mobile Services (Location Service, API Gateway, AWS Amplify)	AI, ML, and IoT Services (Amazon SageMaker (ML), Amazon Forecast(AI), Amazon Fraud Detector (AI))

Figure 16.3 AWS platform services

Next, we have platform services that leverage AWS Global Cloud Infrastructure and Foundation Services. In the platform services, let's look at AWS services which are under the database category.

Databases

AWS has a relational database service which is called RDS. We can launch relational databases such as Oracle, MySQL, PostgreSQL, SQLServer on the AWS platform.

AWS also has its NoSQL database service, for example, DynamoDB. Additionally, AWS has caching services such as ElastiCache, Redis which are AWS cache services offering.

Analytics

Under the Analytic category, AWS has an EMR (Elastic Map Reduce) service, which essentially includes Hadoop, Spark, Hive, and some other related services.

AWS also has a service called Kinesis for real-time processing, which is a Kafka alternative on AWS. Kafka is an event streaming platform.

AWS also has data warehouse services such as RedShift and many other related services to help build data pipelines on AWS.

App Services

Under application services, quick examples are SES (Simple Email Service), SNS (Simple Notification Service), and many other related services. Deployment and Management

Deployment and Management

Then in the Deployment and Management category, AWS has ECS, which stands for Elastic Container Service. In addition, it has CloudWatch Service for monitoring and logging and many more.

Mobile Services

In Mobile Services, AWS has many services to build deploy apps on Apple's IOS and Google's Android platform, for example, Location service, API gateway, AWS Amplify, and many more.

AI, ML, and IoT

AWS also has a rich set of services to build AI, ML, and Internet of things related applications. For example, Amazon SageMaker in machine learning, in AI, Amazon Comprehend for advanced text analytics, Amazon CodeGuru for automated code reviews, Amazon Forecast for demand forecasting, Amazon Fraud Detector for fraud prevention, and many more.

Enterprise IT Applications

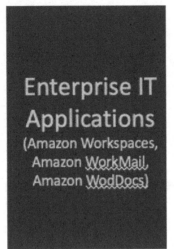

In addition to above all, AWS also has services in the Enterprise IT Applications category, for example, Amazon Workspaces, Amazon WorkMail, and Amazon WordDocs. These applications for corporate email & calendaring, document collaboration, and virtual desktops make it easy to meet employees' usability, performance & reliability expectations and help improve sharing and collaboration.

This was a very high-level overview of some popular AWS services in different categories or types. This should help you wrap up the idea about how various kinds of AWS services fit in the larger scheme of things on the AWS cloud computing platform.

AWS Database Services: High-Level Overview

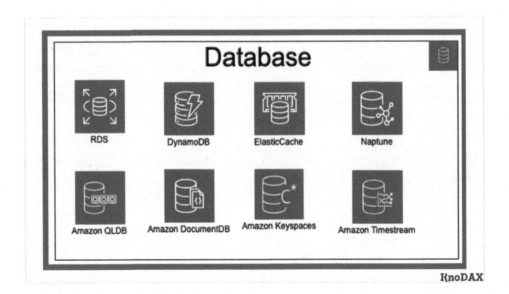

AWS has many database services to help ease doing database-related parts of a project on the cloud. It has RDS, DynamoDB, ElastiCache, Neptune, QLDB, DocumentDB, KeySpaces, and Timestream services in the category.

RDS

The first service in this category is RDS, which is the Relational Database Service. Amazon RDS makes it easy to set up, operate, and scale relational databases in the cloud; for example, using RDS service, you can easily launch Aurora, MySQL, MariaDB, PostgreSQL, Oracle, and Microsoft SQL Server.

Amazon DynamoDB

The next service in this category is Amazon DynamoDB. Basically, DynamoDB is an AWS NoSQL Database Service that applications can use if they have the requirement of consistent, single-digit millisecond latency at any scale. Its flexible data model and reliable performance make it a great fit for many applications such as mobile, web, gaming, AdTech, and IoT.

ElastiCache

The other service in this category is ElastiCache. Essentially this is an in-memory cache service of AWS. It makes it easier to launch, manage, and scale distributed in-memory cache in the cloud.

Amazon Neptune

The other service in this category is Amazon Neptune, which is essentially an AWS Graph database service. Neptune Graph Database service makes it easy to build and run applications that work with highly connected datasets.

Amazon QLDB

The next service in the database category is Amazon QLDB, a ledger database with immutable and cryptographically verifiable transaction logs. For example, the Journal contains the current state and all the lineage of the history.

Say, for example, if you bought a new car and have it registered to the DMV. If you used Amazon QLDB, there would be two parts: one is the current state of the car, for example, who is the current owner, registration plate number, etc. And the other will be all transactions as immutable records will be stored. So, any time you can query the ledger database for the current state and all the historical lineage of the change records.

Amazon DocumentDB

The next service is Amazon DocumentDB. Essentially if you are looking for MongoDB on AWS, please use this service. It is a fast, scalable, highly available, and fully managed document database service that supports MongoDB workloads.

Amazon Keyspaces

The next service is Amazon Keyspaces. This is managed, scalable, highly available Apache Cassandra compatible database service. So if you are looking for Apache Cassandra NoSQL database service on AWS, this is your service.

Amazon TimeStream

And the last service in the database category is Amazon TimeStream. It is a fast, scalable, and serverless time series database service. So, if you have a use case in which, for example, you need to quickly analyze time-series data generated by IoT applications using built-in analytic functions such as smoothing, approximation, and interpolation, Amazon TimeStream is your solution choice on AWS.

AWS Analytics Services: High-Level Overview

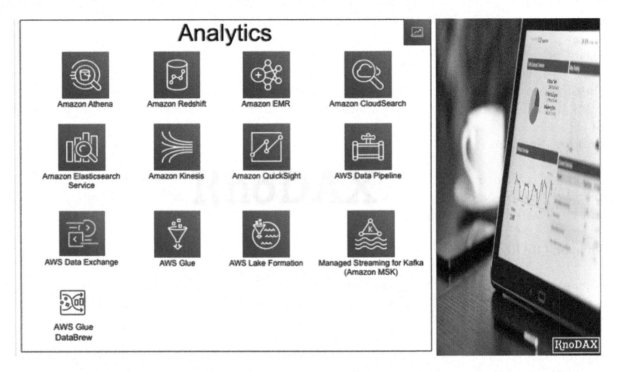

The AWS platform provides many useful analytics services to help perform different types of analysis and insights using all types of data such as big data, unstructured, semi-structured, and structured data.

Amazon Athena Service

Let's start with the Amazon Athena service. Athena is a serverless analytic service. Serverless means you don't need to set up or manage any infrastructure to use the service. Furthermore, Athena is an interactive query service to analyze data directly on S3 by using standard SQL.

So, what would be a typical use case of Athena? If your use case is to query data on S3 for ad-hoc analysis, use the Amazon Athena service.

Amazon RedShift Service

The next one is the Amazon Redshift service. Amazon Redshift is an AWS data warehouse solution where you can query and load exabytes of structured and semi-structured data. The Redshift service is fast and scalable. Furthermore, It is simple to use as you use standard SQL. Additionally, It is cost-effective as well.

So, if your use case requires running simple and cost-effective analytic across massive structured and semi-structure data, the Amazon RedShift service could be a good solution choice.

Amazon EMR Service

Another one is the Amazon EMR service. You can think of EMR as Hadoop and Spark cluster solution on the cloud. So, If you have a use case that requires Hadoop or Spark cluster on AWS, this is your service.

Amazon CloudSearch Service

The next service is the Amazon CloudSearch service. Amazon CloudSearch is an AWS solution to search documents. For example, if you have a use case where you would like to have your documents searchable, this service could be a good solution choice.

Amazon Elasticsearch Service

Another service is Amazon Elasticsearch. The Elasticsearch service is also a solution to search documents similar to CloudSearch. There are some differences, though.

The main highlighted difference is that CloudSearch is a managed service. In other words, in CloudSearch, you don't need to set up and manage servers. On the other hand, for the Elasticsearch service, you will have to set up and manage servers to use the service.

Amazon Kinesis Service

The next analytic category service is the Amazon Kinesis service. The Kinesis service essentially collects, process, and analyze data streams in real-time. Moreover, it is a collection of three services: Kinesis Data Streams, Kinesis Data Firehose, and Kinesis Data Analytics.

So, If you have a use case of real-time data ingestion and consumption on AWS, you will look for Kinesis.

Amazon QuickSight Service

The next is QuickSight service. Amazon QuickSight is a fast business analytic service. It makes it easy for you to build visualizations, perform ad-hoc analysis on uploaded files.

Additionally, you can also perform analysis on databases like SQL Server, MySql, and PostgreSQL. Furthermore, you can perform analysis by ingesting data on Amazon RDS, Redshift, or S3.

So, if you have a use case that requires building and sharing analytic dashboard(s) using data sets from files, databases, RDS, Redshift, or S3, Quicksight is your solution choice.

Amazon Data Pipeline Service

Another analytic category service is the Data Pipeline service. It helps you move, integrate, and process data across AWS compute and storage resources, including on-premises resources.

As a result, this service can be used to build an ETL data pipeline. So, if your use case is to build an ETL data pipeline, the AWS Data Pipeline service could be a good solution choice.

Amazon Data Exchange Service

The next service is AWS Data Exchange. AWS Data Exchange is a compelling analytic service to build analytic or ML solutions. It does it by finding, subscribing, and using data sets from more than 80 qualified data providers.

For example, the service uses data from Reuters, TransUnion, IMDb, Pitney Bowes, etc. So, if you have a use case to build an analytic or ML solution by using data from multiple sources, this is your solution service.

Amazon Glue Service

The next service is AWS Glue. AWS Glue is a serverless data integration service that you can leverage to build analytic or ML solutions.

The best part of the AWS Glue -- in my opinion -- is its flexibility, features, and connectivity to various AWS services.

For example, it allows you to develop Spark jobs using Scala and Python by connecting to different data sources. In addition to this, you can also configure jobs to schedule to run as ETL data pipelines. Essentially, you can build and also schedule ETL jobs using AWS Glue.

Amazon Lake Formation Service

The next AWS analytic category service is AWS Lake Formation. AWS Lake Formation makes it much easier to build data lakes. Instead of building data lakes in months, you can build in days from a dashboard with just a few clicks.

You point to data lake formation at the data sources that you want to move into lake formation. And AWS does the heavy lifting of crawling the schemas and setting up the right metadata tags.

Additionally, it can also perform cleaning, partitioning, indexing, and deduping the data. As a result, storing and accessing data becomes cost-effective and quick.

Finally, Lake Formation helps data analysts and data scientists as it actually puts in a catalog in a much easier to manage way.

Amazon Managed Streaming for Apache Kafka

Another AWS service is Amazon Managed Streaming for Apache Kafka, also called Amazon MSK. Essentially MSK is a fully managed, highly available, and secure Kafka Service.

When using MSK, you will not have the operational overhead of managing Kafka's environment. Additionally, MSK manages the provisioning, configuration, and maintenance of resources within MSK clusters.

So, If you have a use case where you need to build Kafka applications on AWS, you can use MSK.

AWS Glue DataBrew

And the final analytics type service on the list -- as of this recording -- is AWS Glue DataBrew. AWS Glue DataBrew is a visual data preparation tool that enables users to clean and normalize data without writing any code. It has around 250 pre-built transformations to automate data preparation tasks.

Related YouTube Video
AWS Cloud Computing Platform: https://youtu.be/qaKW0AHP9xg

Chapter Review Questions

For the questions given below, please mark them if they are true or false.

1. EC2 is used to launch virtual machines on the cloud – these launched virtual machines are called EC2 instances. True / False

2. AWS has S3 – Simple Storage Service -- an object storage service. True / False

3. AWS IAM service -- Identity and Access Management service-- is used to manage users, groups, and their permissions. True / False

4. We can launch relational databases such as Oracle, MySQL, PostgreSQL, SQLServer on the AWS platform. True / False

5. Which is the AWS proprietary NoSQL database service? True / False

6. AWS ECS -- Elastic Container Service -- is a Docker alternative on AWS. True / False

Please select the correct answer from the given choices for the questions below.

7. Which of the following AWS services is like Apache Kafka on AWS?

    a. EMR
    b. SQS
    c. Kinesis
    d. SES

8. Which of the following options is the AWS data warehouse service?

    a. DynamoDB
    b. RedShift
    c. Kinesis

d. RDS

9. You would like to launch a fully managed MySQL compatible database on AWS platform. Which of the following AWS Services will you use?

    a. Open Source MySQL
    b. Oracle MySQL
    c. Amazon Aurora
    d. Amazon Neptune

10. Which of the following options is an AWS NoSQL Database Service?

    a. MongoDB
    b. CouchDB
    c. NeptuneDB
    d. DynamoDB

11. Which of the following options is an AWS Graph Database?

    a. Amazon GraphDB
    b. Amazon Neptune
    c. Amazon QLDB
    d. Amazon RDS

12. Which of the following AWS services will you use to implement a ledger database with immutable and cryptographically verifiable transaction logs?

    a. Amazon GraphDB
    b. Amazon Neptune
    c. Amazon QLDB
    d. Amazon RDS

13. You are looking for a MongoDB type document database service on AWS platform. Which of the following AWS services will you use for document databases?

    a. Amazon DocumentDB
    b. Amazon DynamoDB
    c. Amazon Neptune
    d. Amazon QLDB

14. You are looking for Cassandra compatible NoSQL database service on the AWS platform. Which of the following AWS services will you use for Cassandra compatible databases?

    a. Amazon DocumentDB
    b. Amazon DynamoDB
    c. Amazon Neptune
    d. Amazon KeySpaces

15. You are looking for time series service on AWS platform. Which of the following AWS services will you use on AWS to implement time series?

    a. Amazon KeySpaces
    b. Amazon DynamoDB
    c. Amazon Neptune
    d. Amazon TimeStream

16. You have been asked to run SQL on S3 to perform some analytic operations. Which of the following AWS services can you use to run SQL on S3?

    a. Amazon MySQL
    b. Amazon Aurora
    c. Amazon Athena
    d. Amazon Neptune

17. Your use case requires analyzing petabytes of structured and semi-structured data. Which of the following AWS services would be a better choice for the given use case?

    a. Amazon Athena
    b. Amazon RedShift
    c. Amazon RDS
    d. Amazon DynamoDB

18. Your use case requires to setting up a Hadoop cluster to run Spark jobs on the AWS platform. Which of the following AWS services will you use for the given use case?

    a. Amazon Athena
    b. Amazon RedShift
    c. Amazon Kinesis
    d. Amazon EMR

19. Your use case requires set up a Hadoop cluster to run Spark jobs on the AWS platform. Which of the following AWS services will you use for the given use case?

    a. Amazon Athena
    b. Amazon RedShift
    c. Amazon Kinesis
    d. Amazon EMR

20. Your use case requires real-time data ingestion on AWS. Which of the following AWS services will you use to ingest real-time data on the AWS platform?

    a. Amazon Athena
    b. Amazon RedShift
    c. Amazon Kinesis
    d. Amazon EMR

21. Your use case requires writing Spark jobs against data files stored on S3 and then setting up a data pipeline to get analytics on the data. Which of the following AWS services will you use?

    a. Amazon RedShift
    b. Amazon EMR
    c. AWS Glue
    d. Amazon Lake Formation

Chapter 17: Cost-Benefit Analysis

"Unexpected kindness is the most powerful, least costly, and most underrated agent of human change." -- Bob Kerrey

◆◆◆

You have gone through many chapters about cloud computing and AWS with a great deal of understanding of cloud computing. This chapter is about cost-benefit analysis. There is a saying nothing comes free in the world. Though, AWS provides Free Tier, which is very extensive; however, AWS Free Tier cannot be used as a production load. There are many possible advantages to transferring to a cloud platform, depending on how large and old the organization is. Any organization migrating to a cloud or start-ups thinking to adopt cloud must undertake cost-benefit analysis before taking the final decision.

The cloud may be a very cost-effective option. However, migrating to a cloud environment may not be the right choice if the organization is in tight regulatory constraints or if its existing applications are not ready for the cloud because of architectural coupling or not designed to be easily portable to a cloud environment. There may be other options, in that case, to migrate to a cloud such as a hybrid cloud or a private cloud.

Let's focus our discussion on the cost-benefit analysis of moving to a public cloud, as this is one of the main reasons the cloud computing paradigm has become so popular.

Cyclical or Seasoned Demand

Some organizations have cyclical demand for more high-end resources to manage load peaks. For example, organizations in the e-commence domain tend to have more traffic during the holiday season. On the same token, news or media organizations also have a similar scenario where organizations' websites get more traffic if some newsworthy events happen. Generally, to handle seasonal or unexpected demand, organizations buy and maintain additional servers to make sure that their applications are scalable to distribute the load on these additional servers.

As you can see that organizations have two challenges here. The number one is an extra upfront cost of buying IT resources such as servers and then maintaining them. And the next is, it's a bit challenging to predict future traffic. In a growing business situation, they may have to keep buying and keeping additional servers each time to manage the new additional demand. Would that be enough? What if there are budget issues? What if the business scenario changed and traffic decreased-- then, the bought servers would be sitting idle, and invested capital expenditure -- also called CapEx-- in purchasing those servers would provide little benefit to the organization. Managing scalability in an on-premises environment is like chasing a dog's tail from the capital expenditure perspective. There is a strong possibility of resources sitting idle in regular or off-peak hours. This discussion was from a CapEx (Capital Expenditure) perspective. Let's discuss this from an operational expenditure (OpEx) aspect.

Buying additional servers increase maintenance and operation cost as well. System admin or IT admin staff will require to take the work of maintaining additional servers. Organizations may have to hire and add more system admin or operations staff to manage and support additional servers. This would lead to an increase in operating expenses or OpEx.

We got an understanding of CapEx and OpEx challenges in an on-premises environment. Let's see how organizations can address the scalability issue (handling cyclical demand or unexpected demand that can pop up anytime in the case of news or media organizations) of managing demand in the cloud computing paradigm. Since the cloud platform provides virtually unlimited resources, organizations can seamlessly drive unexpected or seasoned traffic and pay for operational expenses (OpEx). As you can see that the cloud platform is handy in handling

Cloud Computing and AWS Introduction

scalability issues just by paying for operations (operational expenditure). In fact, on the cloud platform, there is no capital expenditure for the deployed applications, as cloud providers bear the cost of setting up, running, and maintaining servers on their cloud platform.

Change in Focus

Even though there is no direct cost-benefit of change in focus, however, it's essential to discuss this aspect with respect to migrating to the cloud. Let's see the situation or environment before moving to the cloud.

The transition to the cloud for the organization, which has had an on-premises environment for quite a long time, may not be that easy. Transitioning to the cloud may create uneasiness in employees who run and maintain systems. When the transition is made, their role will be more of overseeing the operation than the direct involvement. And other employees and the department may also have similar uneasiness towards the transition to the cloud. Migration to the cloud in a rush may cause unhealthy environments such as productivity disruption, internal fighting, employees leaving the organization. On the other hand, many other employees may be very excited and interested in the transition as they may learn new technology and new skills.

The most significant change that happens with respect to change in focus is employees would be more creative in doing proof of concepts type projects or taking new projects. Project managers would also find migration to the cloud much helpful as the IT resource needed for the development is much faster -- in almost no time. All development engineers need is an AWS account and the necessary permission to access cloud resources.

Ownership and Control

Organizations in an on-prem data center scenario have complete control of everything -- hardware, operating system, software, and data. This control is very advantageous with the freedom to manage every aspect of IT. However, in the case of cloud migration, the ownership and control parts are shared with the cloud provider.

Nonetheless, cloud providers such as AWS provide lots of flexibility in controlling the system and handling baseline security, which is better than data centers – which is, for the most part, about just renting rack space for servers.

Cost Predictability

In an on-prem data center environment, not only does the organization has in control hardware, software, and data, but the organization has a predicable cost – the cost of physical IT infrastructure, cost of running and maintaining the IT infrastructure. This predictability is changed totally in the cloud environment.

Cloud Computing and AWS Introduction

In general, the cloud is known for variable pricing – metered cost. This is because organizations pay based on the usage of resources. This variable or unpredictably type of cost may not be a right for some finance or budget departments of some organizations. Nonetheless, cloud providers have different pricing options, such as reserved instances that can bring more predictability to the cloud expenditure cost (OpEx).

How Does Moving to Cloud Help Reduce Costs?

Right-Sized Infrastructure

In general, most of the on-premises are overprovisioned. According to one research (http://tsologic.com/resources/economics-of-cloud-migration-2017/)more than 80% of on-premises workloads are overprovisioned. There could be a reason behind that. Often, organizations buy server infrastructure to meet the demand of current workloads and the anticipated demands of future workloads. If the workloads need don't increase, the servers run as overprovisioned. This is not a good use of business capital, as you can realize.

When businesses move to the cloud, they can take advantage of its agility and flexibility features. The agility and flexibility lead to leaner delivery processes and thus help cut overall IT infrastructure costs. You can provision resources on-demand on the cloud – no need to overprovision. As the demand for workloads increases, you can provision more resources and de-provision if you don't need them. You can do it manually or automatically using auto-scaling and elasticity features to manage right-size provisioning automatically.

Essentially, a cloud platform can help run your workloads with the right-size infrastructure – no need to over-provision or under-provision the resources.

Utilizing Automation Strategies

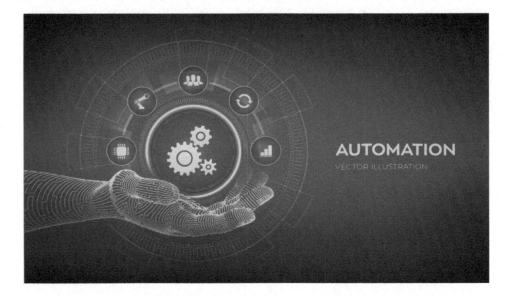

Migrating to the cloud reduces the cost of setting up, running, and managing IT infrastructure by leveraging automation. For example, engineers can write scripts to automate backup, storage, code deployment, settings, and configurations. These automation tasks reduce the amount of human intervention needed and allow IT staff to focus on critical business priorities. This is one aspect of saving costs with automation – reducing human intervention. Another aspect of automation is dynamically provisioning and de-provisioning of needed resources -- *right size (no over-provision or under-provision)*.

Automation is a significant cost-reducing factor in the cloud. AWS has a vast source of APIs to automate almost most of AW'S services without managing them using AWS Management Console.

Reduce in Security and Compliance Scope

AWS has a concept of the Shared Responsibility Model. Regarding security and compliance, it means responsibilities are shared between AWS customers and AWS. When migrating to the cloud, this is excellent news as organizations' scope of managing security and compliance is reduced when moving to the cloud; for example, the physical security of IT resources is taken care of by AWS. However, in the Shared Responsibility Model, you still will have lots of control over customers' data and how it will be stored and encrypted -- at rest or in transit.

Managed services

AWS managed services -- from database to analytic and logging and monitoring -- provide significant cost savings when moving to the cloud. In addition, these services help reduce operational costs -- coupled with the pay-as-you-go model, the managed services offer flexibility to businesses.

Let's take an example, suppose that you need to store master lookup tables data in an Oracle database with a maximum of 20 tables. If you were to compare it with buying an Oracle license just to store data for master lookup tables vs. using AWS RDS service – you would probably be inclined to use the RDS service. Cost savings from managed services are a significant component for many essential and ad-hoc type operations.

References:
- https://aws.amazon.com/blogs/enterprise-strategy/rightsizing-infrastructure-can-cut-costs-36/
- https://voleer.com/blog/2019/9/17/reduce-your-cloud-costs-with-these-5-strategies
- http://tsologic.com/resources/economics-of-cloud-migration-2017/

Appendix

Scope of Responsibility

As we know software doesn't run in isolation – it needs server, storage, operating system, virtualization (if virtual machines are used), networking, database (if the application requires). Software needs to be managed from its performance aspects such as scalability. In addition, it needs to be secured as well – depending on the security needs of the application.

That being the case, responsibilities of the different runtime aspects of the application: who will manage what depends. In the on-premises datacenter deployment, the software owner takes responsibility for the application in its entirety. The dependency of the application's runtime environment is managed and controlled by the software owner. In the case of a cloud deployment, this responsibility, however, changes. The responsibility is shared between the cloud provider and the application owner. What aspect of the application's runtime environment is managed by the cloud provider and what aspects are to be managed by the application owner – depends on the cloud computing type leveraged by the application. Is the application using IaaS, or is it using PaaS, or is the application a SaaS application?

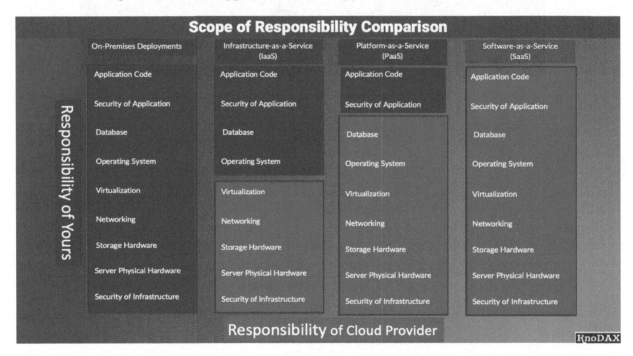

As you can notice in the picture, in the case of on-premises deployments, each aspect such as physical hardware, software, networking, and security of the application needs to be managed and controlled by the software owner. At the other end -- in the case of using SaaS applications of the cloud provider -- all these aspects are managed and controlled by the cloud provider.

If the application is using IaaS or PaaS, the responsibilities are divided between the application owner and the cloud provider. In the case of IaaS, the cloud provider is responsible for physical hardware, storage, networking, virtualization; and the application owner is responsible for the operating system, database, application code, and security of the application. In the case of

PaaS, only application code and application's security fall on the application owner, and the rest of the other responsibilities are taken care of by the cloud provider.

Elasticity

In cloud computing, you will come across the term *elastic* a lot. For example, AWS has many services that include the term *elastic* in its name, for example, Elastic Compute Cloud, Elastic Load Balancer, Elastic Block Storage, Elastic MapReduce.

The term *elastic* in cloud computing is sort of analogous to an elastic band. You can stretch an elastic band size beyond its rest state; and when you let it go, it will come back to its resting size. This elastic concept -- going back to its resting size when we let it go from its stretched state -- is extremely useful in cloud computing.

Let me share with you an anecdote related to elasticity. When I was learning AWS in 2013, I set up a web server of three machines with an Elastic Load Balancer. I had set up scalability to launch additional machines when CPU utilization reaches more than 70% (just demo the 70% doesn't have any significance here as this was just a learning exercise). As the webserver was running and EC2 instances were running, I was not paying attention (forgot to set up a billing alert -- very new to AWS) to my AWS billing dashboard. When the billing cycle ended, I got the billing email from AWS. I was surprised to notice a bill of around $40.00. Since I was using AWS Free Tier, this bill seemed to be a little much. When I looked up in detail, I noticed that an additional webserver was getting launched when the CPU utilization was above 70%, but the server was terminating when CPU utilization was less than 70%. The reason was that I had not configured to make it elastic – terminate when the CPU utilization goes below 70%. I had to call AWS support and explain the situation. The good news was they removed that extra charge from the bill – thank you, AWS! Later, I added the configuration to terminate the EC2 instance if the CPU utilization goes below 70%. And the problem was fixed – the webserver set up configuration was made *elastic*.

I think you got the idea from the above anecdote, that AWS elastic services scale up the resources to handle the additional load to maintain the expected performance level. And conversely, when the load decreases, they terminate or scale down the additional resources when the resources are not needed.

Let's take an example to understand the term elastic as it relates to cloud computing on AWS. The hypothetical use case is related to setting up a scalable web server. We set up the webserver with a minimum of 3, and a maximum of 6 EC2 instances. Each EC2 instance will be launched using a custom AMI to launch Apache webserver. We have also configured AWS Elastic Load Balancer to launch additional EC2 instances if CPU utilization for an EC2 instance reaches above 70% on AWS Cloud Watch – maximum up to six instances. And terminate the EC2 instance when the CPU utilization comes down to less than 70% -- minimum up to three instances. As you can see, we have set up a scalable and -- elastic -- web server.

References

1. https://docs.aws.amazon.com/AWSEC2/latest/UserGuide/concepts.html

2. https://aws.amazon.com/autoscaling/

3. https://aws.amazon.com/s3/

4. https://aws.amazon.com/ebs/

5. https://aws.amazon.com/iam/

6. https://docs.aws.amazon.com/vpc/latest/userguide/VPC_Internet_Gateway.html

7. https://aws.amazon.com/directconnect/

8. https://aws.amazon.com/rds/

9. https://aws.amazon.com/elasticache/

10. https://aws.amazon.com/redis/

11. https://aws.amazon.com/emr/

12. https://aws.amazon.com/kinesis/

13. https://aws.amazon.com/ses/

14. https://aws.amazon.com/sns

15. https://aws.amazon.com/ecs/

16. https://aws.amazon.com/location/

17. https://aws.amazon.com/api-gateway/

18. https://aws.amazon.com/amplify/

19. https://aws.amazon.com/sagemaker/

20. https://aws.amazon.com/workspaces/

21. https://aws.amazon.com/workmail/

22. https://aws.amazon.com/workdocs/

23. https://aws.amazon.com/about-aws/global-infrastructure/regions_az/

24. https://en.wikipedia.org/wiki/Cloud_computing

25.   https://www.backblaze.com/blog/vm-vs-containers/

26.   https://www.ibm.com/cloud/blog/containers-vs-vms

27.   https://www.vxchnge.com/blog/different-types-of-cloud-computing

28.   https://www.cloudflare.com/learning/serverless/what-is-serverless/

29.   https://aws.amazon.com/serverless/

30.   https://www.ibm.com/cloud/learn/serverless

31.   https://dzone.com/articles/serverless-services-on-aws-an-overview

32.   https://docs.docker.com/desktop/mac/install/

33.   https://docs.docker.com/desktop/windows/install/

34.   https://www.zdnet.com/article/using-google-authenticator-heres-why-you-should-get-rid-of-it/

35.   https://hub.docker.com/

36.   https://docs.docker.com/engine/reference/commandline/docker/

37.   https://en.wikipedia.org/wiki/Multi-factor_authentication

38.   https://www.aboutamazon.com/news/aws/partnering-with-the-nfl-to-transform-player-health-and-safety

39.   https://www.contino.io/insights/whos-using-aws

40.   https://press.aboutamazon.com/news-releases/news-release-details/twitter-selects-aws-strategic-provider-serve-timelines

41.   https://docs.aws.amazon.com/whitepapers/latest/aws-overview/security-and-compliance.html

42.   https://www.zdnet.com/article/using-google-authenticator-heres-why-you-should-get-rid-of-it/

43.   https://www.youtube.com/watch?v=0R23JRR671I

44.   https://www.reddit.com/r/askscience/comments/5imnis/how_do_gemalto_tokens_work_curious_how_the_system/

Congratulations on completing this book! I hope you found this book helpful.

The book is intended to help you understand cloud computing and AWS from an introductory perspective. If you enjoyed this book and felt that the book was helpful to add value to your life, we ask you to please take the time to review it.

Your honest feedback is highly appreciated. It does make a difference!
If you noticed any problem, please let us know by emailing us at support@knodax.com before writing any review online. It will be beneficial for us to improve the quality of our books.

Made in the USA
Coppell, TX
02 August 2022

80761990R00131